EYEWITNESS  GUIDES

BOAT

"Jolly Roger"
pirate flag

South American reed raft

19th-century Dutch canal boat

Ship's wheel

Portuguese "half moon"
fishing boat

18th-century Delftware figure
of sailor's farewell

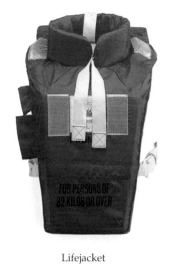
Lifejacket

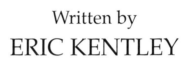
EYEWITNESS GUIDES

BOAT

Ship's bell

Written by
ERIC KENTLEY

Chinese junk
from Foochow

Three-island tramp steamer

Commemorative plate showing
ship launch

Barque in a bottle

DORLING KINDERSLEY
London • New York • Stuttgart
in association with
THE NATIONAL MARITIME MUSEUM

River boat propeller

Compass card from a
19th-century Russian ship

French ship's
figurehead

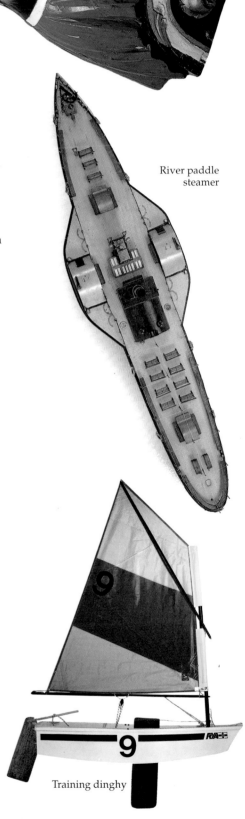

River paddle
steamer

Training dinghy

Shop sign of a midshipman
with a quadrant

DK

A DORLING KINDERSLEY BOOK

Project editor Scott Steedman
Art editor Martin Atcherley
Senior editor Helen Parker
Senior art editor Julia Harris
Production Louise Barratt
Picture research Deborah Pownall
Special photography James Stevenson and
Tina Chambers of the National Maritime Museum

This Eyewitness ® Guide has been conceived by
Dorling Kindersley Limited
and Editions Gallimard

First published in Great Britain in 1992 by
Dorling Kindersley Limited,
9 Henrietta Street, London WC2E 8PS

Reprinted 1996

Copyright © 1992 Dorling Kindersley Limited,
London

A CIP catalogue record for this book is available
from the British Library

ISBN 0 86318 793 5

Colour reproduction by Colourscan, Singapore
Printed in Singapore by Toppan

Contents

Four-masted ship *Wendur*

6
Taking to the water
8
Rafts
10
Skin boats
12
Bark canoes
14
Dugouts and outriggers
16
Plank boats
18
Putting planks together
20
Oarsome power
22
Blowing in the wind
24
Sail style
26
The Age of Sail
30
Thar' she blows!
32
A splash of colour
34
In sheltered waters
36
Steam and paddlewheels
38
Turn of the screw

40
Last days of the merchant sail
42
Hook, line, and sinker
46
Building in iron and steel
48
Tramping the seas
50
In the dock
52
On the bridge
54
Luxurious liners
58
S.O.S. (Save Our Souls!)
60
Yachts for cruising
62
Learning the ropes
64
Index

Taking to the water

To explore, to travel, to trade, to fish, to fight, and for fun – people take to the water for all these reasons. For thousands of years, they have been developing new ways to make being on the water easier, safer, and quicker. The earliest craft were simple rafts and floats. But then the hollow shell which sat on the water – probably a hollowed log – was invented. This was the boat, an invention as important as the wheel. Still used all over the world, the wooden boat is the ancestor of the great sailing ships and the huge ferries and container ships of today. There are now many hundreds of different types of boat and ship, made from every material imaginable, from reeds or animal skins to plastic, fibreglass, iron, and steel.

ASSYRIAN AMPHIBIAN
This Ancient Assyrian is literally floating on air. He is sitting astride an animal skin which has been blown up with air to make a simple float. The Assyrians were using log rafts, boats made from animal skins (pp. 10–11), and floats like this one for fishing, crossing rivers, and transporting wood, at least 2,600 years ago.

WHAT IS A SHIP?
All large vessels are usually called ships, but this word also has a precise meaning. A ship has three or more masts all rigged with square sails. The *Kruzenshtern's* fourth mast has fore-and-aft sails (pp. 24–25), which makes her a "barque", not a ship.

FALLING OFF A LOG
Thousands of years ago, a floating log may have given someone the idea of making the first floating vessel. This boy on a log is punting – standing up and pushing a pole against the bottom of the river or lake. But except in the calmest water, the log's shape will make it roll, throwing him off. It can be made stable by tying another log to it to form a raft. Or the log can be hollowed out, to make a boat. This is more stable because the weight of the passenger is lower down.

FLOATING TENDER
There is no clear distinction between a boat and a ship, but you can say a boat can be put on a ship, but a ship can't be put on a boat! This is a "tender", a small boat used to ferry people and goods between a ship (or a bigger boat) and the shore. It is made of wooden planks, though boats can be made of anything that can be formed into a hollow shell.

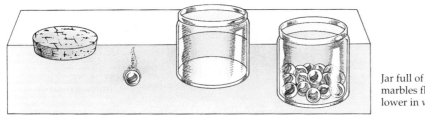

Cork floats Glass marble sinks Glass jar floats

Jar full of marbles floats lower in water

WHY DO THINGS FLOAT?

It all depends on density – the mass of an object divided by its volume. Materials like cork float because they are less dense than water. A glass marble sinks because it is denser than water. But a glass jar full of air will float because its density is made much lower by the air inside. If marbles are added to it, the jar will still float, at least until its total density is as high as the water. The same is true of a laden steel box – like an oil tanker, for instance.

BULKY CARRIER

Like most modern ships, this "bulk carrier" is too big and cumbersome to manoeuvre in a harbour under its own steam. Instead she (all ships are usually called "she") is being pushed and pulled by tugs. Some bulk carriers can carry over 200,000 tonnes of cargo. But they are small compared to most oil tankers, which can carry twice as much.

PLANING HULL

This is the great Italian pilot Antonio Becchi winning the 1934 12-litre powerboat race at Palm Beach in the USA. When it is moving fast, the engine of a powerboat forces the bow up slightly so that the boat "planes", skims, across the surface of the water.

Mast

Yard

Yard

Mast

Shroud

Sail

Stay

Bowsprit, to hold sails at bow

Boom

Tiller

Rudder

Hull, the main body of a boat or ship

Keel

TALKING ABOUT BOATS

Boats and ships have their own language and special names for many of their parts. The front or "fore" of a boat is called the bow; the back or "aft" is the stern. Long ago, the steering board which was used to guide a boat was held on the right side, which became known as "starboard". The left side is called "port". This yacht, *America*, is a typical sailing boat. She has a keel, to stop her being blown sideways by the wind; masts, yards, and booms to carry her sails; and shrouds and stays to hold up her masts. She is steered by a rudder which is moved by the tiller.

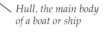

WHAT IS NOT A BOAT?

Though it travels across water, a hovercraft is not a boat or a raft because it does not come into contact with the water. It sits on a cushion of air about 20 cm (8 in) above the surface with its whirring propellers pushing air, not water.

Rafts

Driftwood, logs, reeds, bags of air – rafts can be made from anything which is light enough to float with people on board. They are probably the oldest form of water transport. Unlike boats, rafts are not watertight structures; they float because of the natural buoyancy of their materials. This means that while you can usually sit *in* a boat, you have to sit (or stand) *on* a raft. Rafts are found all over the world in many shapes and sizes. In Canada and Russia, huge rafts are formed by lashing large numbers of logs together, simply as a way of moving timber down rivers. Log rafts are still used as fishing craft in many areas. Because they let in water, and the crew can expect to get wet, rafts are more common in warm countries. They may look simple, but rafts are often very carefully shaped to do a particular job on the waters where they work.

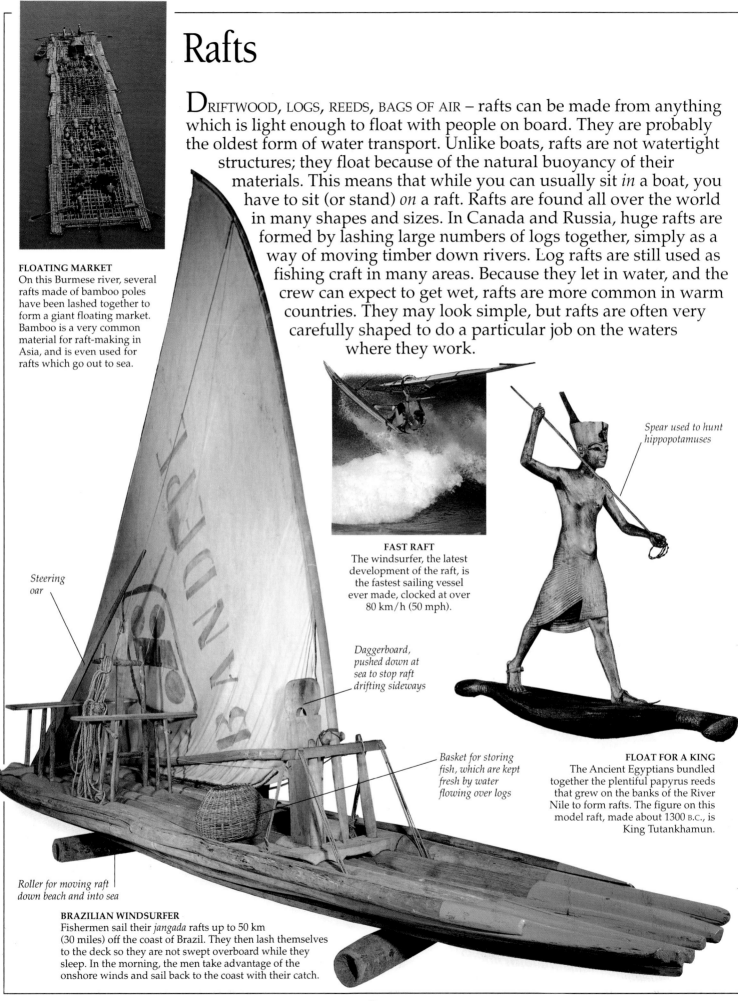

FLOATING MARKET
On this Burmese river, several rafts made of bamboo poles have been lashed together to form a giant floating market. Bamboo is a very common material for raft-making in Asia, and is even used for rafts which go out to sea.

Steering oar

FAST RAFT
The windsurfer, the latest development of the raft, is the fastest sailing vessel ever made, clocked at over 80 km/h (50 mph).

Spear used to hunt hippopotamuses

Daggerboard, pushed down at sea to stop raft drifting sideways

Basket for storing fish, which are kept fresh by water flowing over logs

FLOAT FOR A KING
The Ancient Egyptians bundled together the plentiful papyrus reeds that grew on the banks of the River Nile to form rafts. The figure on this model raft, made about 1300 B.C., is King Tutankhamun.

Roller for moving raft down beach and into sea

BRAZILIAN WINDSURFER
Fishermen sail their *jangada* rafts up to 50 km (30 miles) off the coast of Brazil. They then lash themselves to the deck so they are not swept overboard while they sleep. In the morning, the men take advantage of the onshore winds and sail back to the coast with their catch.

8

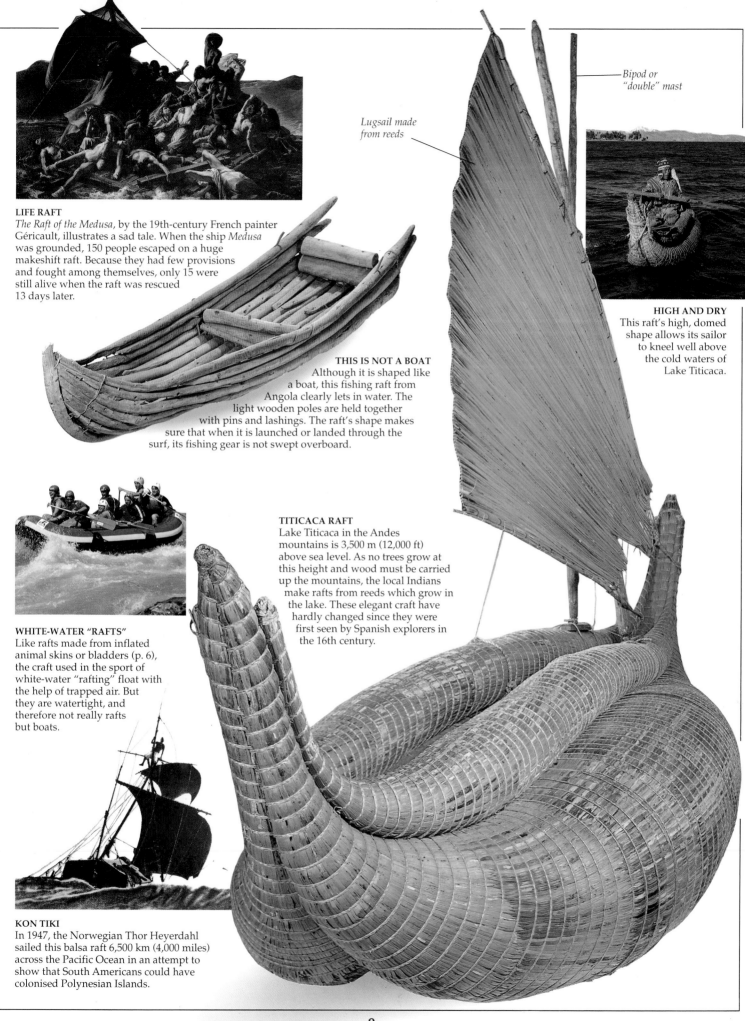

LIFE RAFT
The Raft of the Medusa, by the 19th-century French painter Géricault, illustrates a sad tale. When the ship *Medusa* was grounded, 150 people escaped on a huge makeshift raft. Because they had few provisions and fought among themselves, only 15 were still alive when the raft was rescued 13 days later.

Lugsail made from reeds

Bipod or "double" mast

HIGH AND DRY
This raft's high, domed shape allows its sailor to kneel well above the cold waters of Lake Titicaca.

THIS IS NOT A BOAT
Although it is shaped like a boat, this fishing raft from Angola clearly lets in water. The light wooden poles are held together with pins and lashings. The raft's shape makes sure that when it is launched or landed through the surf, its fishing gear is not swept overboard.

TITICACA RAFT
Lake Titicaca in the Andes mountains is 3,500 m (12,000 ft) above sea level. As no trees grow at this height and wood must be carried up the mountains, the local Indians make rafts from reeds which grow in the lake. These elegant craft have hardly changed since they were first seen by Spanish explorers in the 16th century.

WHITE-WATER "RAFTS"
Like rafts made from inflated animal skins or bladders (p. 6), the craft used in the sport of white-water "rafting" float with the help of trapped air. But they are watertight, and therefore not really rafts but boats.

KON TIKI
In 1947, the Norwegian Thor Heyerdahl sailed this balsa raft 6,500 km (4,000 miles) across the Pacific Ocean in an attempt to show that South Americans could have colonised Polynesian Islands.

Skin boats

RAW MATERIALS
In the British Isles, cattle hide was once used to make round boats called coracles. It has since been replaced by canvas or flannel coated with tar.

WRAPPED AROUND A LIGHT WOODEN FRAMEWORK, the hide of an animal makes a watertight boat. All kinds of animal lose their skin for this purpose. In India, buffalo hides are used to build round boats called paracils; in Tibet, sailors are kept dry thanks to yaks. The native people of the North American prairies once crossed rivers in "bull boats" which were wrapped in bison hide. The Inuit of the Arctic cover their kayaks with sealskins, though with the recent rarity of seals most have switched to waterproofed canvas. The design of many skin boats has not changed in centuries. They are often made in places where wood is scarce. They are light, manoeuvrable, and easy to carry, and some are surprisingly safe in wild water.

GOING WITH THE FLOW
The coracle of Wales and England is a one-person boat used for river fishing. The coracler paddles downstream and then has to walk back along the bank carrying the boat on his back.

LIGHT AND SKINNY
Its light framework and cover make the curach easy to carry from the sea to a safe spot high on the beach.

IRISH SEABOAT
The curach is found on the western coast of Ireland, where trees are few and the Atlantic surf is wild. It is built from cattle hides – or in this case a modern substitute, canvas – stretched over a willow frame. Despite its fragile appearance the curach is used for sea fishing and as transport to islands far out of sight of the mainland.

Crossbeam for extra strength

Mast

Rowing thwart (seat)

Bull, a pivoting wood block nailed to oar

Steering oar

Ash-wood oar

BURIED TREASURE
This gold model, found in a buried cache in Ireland, may be of an early curach. It dates from the first century B.C.

Gunwale (top edge of hull) of ash wood

Framework of willow branches lashed together

BUFFALO BOAT
A framework of interwoven slats of split bamboo makes the south Indian paracil strong and rigid. It is covered with several buffalo hides sewn together.

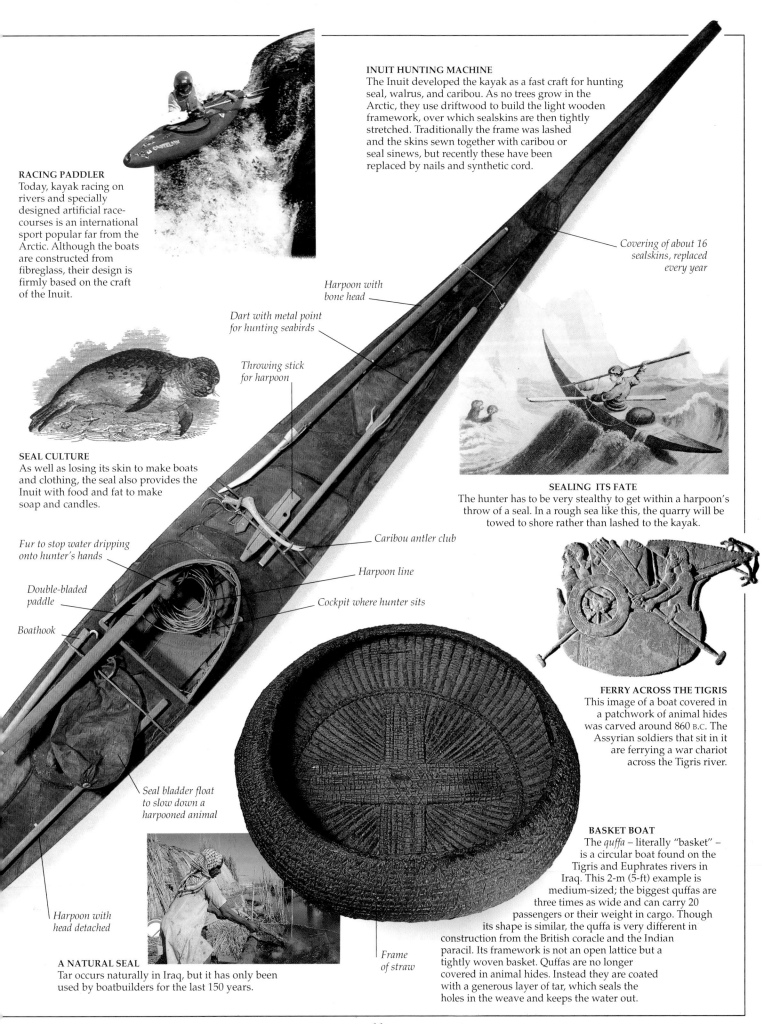

RACING PADDLER
Today, kayak racing on rivers and specially designed artificial race-courses is an international sport popular far from the Arctic. Although the boats are constructed from fibreglass, their design is firmly based on the craft of the Inuit.

INUIT HUNTING MACHINE
The Inuit developed the kayak as a fast craft for hunting seal, walrus, and caribou. As no trees grow in the Arctic, they use driftwood to build the light wooden framework, over which sealskins are then tightly stretched. Traditionally the frame was lashed and the skins sewn together with caribou or seal sinews, but recently these have been replaced by nails and synthetic cord.

Covering of about 16 sealskins, replaced every year

Harpoon with bone head

Dart with metal point for hunting seabirds

Throwing stick for harpoon

SEAL CULTURE
As well as losing its skin to make boats and clothing, the seal also provides the Inuit with food and fat to make soap and candles.

Fur to stop water dripping onto hunter's hands

Double-bladed paddle

Boathook

Caribou antler club

Harpoon line

Cockpit where hunter sits

SEALING ITS FATE
The hunter has to be very stealthy to get within a harpoon's throw of a seal. In a rough sea like this, the quarry will be towed to shore rather than lashed to the kayak.

Seal bladder float to slow down a harpooned animal

Harpoon with head detached

A NATURAL SEAL
Tar occurs naturally in Iraq, but it has only been used by boatbuilders for the last 150 years.

Frame of straw

FERRY ACROSS THE TIGRIS
This image of a boat covered in a patchwork of animal hides was carved around 860 B.C. The Assyrian soldiers that sit in it are ferrying a war chariot across the Tigris river.

BASKET BOAT
The *quffa* – literally "basket" – is a circular boat found on the Tigris and Euphrates rivers in Iraq. This 2-m (5-ft) example is medium-sized; the biggest quffas are three times as wide and can carry 20 passengers or their weight in cargo. Though its shape is similar, the quffa is very different in construction from the British coracle and the Indian paracil. Its framework is not an open lattice but a tightly woven basket. Quffas are no longer covered in animal hides. Instead they are coated with a generous layer of tar, which seals the holes in the weave and keeps the water out.

Bark canoes

Like the skin of an animal, the skin of a tree – its bark – makes a watertight boat. Bark boats have been made in many places, but they were perfected by the people living in the forests of North America. This land is criss-crossed by a vast network of rivers and lakes which holds half of the fresh water in the world. The people here built canoes for gathering wild rice, hunting, transport, and for waging war. The rivers have many rapids, and bark canoes are strong enough to ride rough water. They are also light enough to be carried around waterfalls and really wild stretches. The best bark came from the white paper birch tree, but some canoes were made of elm, chestnut, and even sticky spruce bark. The Europeans who colonised North America were quick to realise the value of the bark canoe for exploration and the fur trade. At first they imitated the native tradition, though these days the art of building in bark is almost dead. But the shape lives on in thousands of canoes mass produced in plastic and fibreglass.

EUCALYPTUS CANOE
The Aboriginal peoples of Australia made canoes from the bark of the eucalyptus tree. This man is standing in one as he fishes in the coastal waters of Tasmania. Bark canoes were also made in Tierra del Fuego at the tip of South America, and in Africa, China, Indonesia, Siberia, and Scandinavia.

SHOOTING THE RAPIDS
For European colonists and tourists, the wilderness of Canada offered unrivalled hunting and fishing, as well as the thrill of riding rough water in a light and flexible boat.

ALGONQUIN CANOE
This birchbark canoe was made by the son of an Algonquin chief. The Algonquin live in the Ottawa Valley and around the many tributaries of the St. Lawrence River, in what is now called Ontario. This is a small example, about 3 m (9 ft) long. Algonquin war canoes were up to 10.5 m (35 ft). They were much faster than the large elm canoes of the Iroquois, a neighbouring people who waged war on the Algonquin.

EXPRESS SERVICE
The Hudson's Bay Company used this 12-m (40-ft) canoe to carry important officials and urgent messages. Among the passengers is Frances Ann Hopkins, the painter of this picture. The normal rate for paddling such a canoe was 40 strokes a minute.

FINISHING TOUCHES
Unlike skin boats, bark boats are made shell first. This canoe shell is nearly finished. The separate pieces of bark are in place and are being sewn together with spruce roots. When this is done, all the sewing holes will be sealed with spruce gum. Then the ribs will be added and the canoe will be ready to float.

STIFFENING
A canoe can be made with no more than an axe and a knife. This woman is carving a rib from a piece of spruce. It will be lashed on the inside to stiffen the canoe's bark shell.

WATER-BORNE HUNTERS
The Chippewa, the biggest tribe in the Great Lakes area, were expert hunters who made canoes for the Hudson's Bay Company. These Chippewa hunters were photographed about 1900.

Cross-strut to strengthen canoe. It is not a seat – the canoeist sits or kneels on the bottom of the boat

Seam sewn with spruce roots and sealed with spruce gum

ONE PIECE
A bottom view shows that this Algonquin canoe is made from a single piece of bark. Larger canoes are made by sewing on extra sheets.

LIGHT AS A CANOE
This detail from a 17th-century French map shows a "portage" (French for "carrying"). This is a detour in a journey in which the canoe is carried overland. Early North American traders and travellers had to make regular portages to avoid rapids or to get from one river system to another.

LEGACY OF BARK
The shape of the bark canoe is so suitable for rough water that it is still copied by plank, plastic, and fibreglass boatbuilders today.

A DAY IN THE LIFE OF THE MICMAC
The Micmac live on the east coast of Canada. Their canoes were closed at the ends so that they could take them to sea and not be swamped by waves. In this scene, painted about 1850, one of the canoes has a sail, an idea (like the guns being used for hunting) taken from European settlers. In earlier times, the Micmac used their canoes to make raids down the coast far to the south.

Dugouts and outriggers

FOR THE LAST 8,000 YEARS, people have been chopping down trees and hollowing them out to make the simplest type of wooden boat – the logboat. The most basic of these "dugout canoes" are roughly made, functional craft just large enough to take one person standing up. Others, like the war canoes made by the Maoris of New Zealand or the Haida tribe of Canada's west coast, can carry 20 people and are beautifully decorated. Because they are heavy and sit low in the water, most logboats are restricted to calm waters. However, in the Pacific, logboats were once used for great journeys across the ocean. On some Pacific islands, two or more logboats are lashed together. But more often a wooden float is fitted to the side of the dugout hull to make a stable and efficient sailing boat, the outrigger canoe.

HOT ROCKS
A hollowed log can be widened by filling it with water, which is brought to the boil by tossing in heated stones. This softens the wood so the sides can be pushed apart.

Large mallet

Two-handed adze for rough shaping

WAR CANOE
Using only stone tools, the Maoris of New Zealand created the world's most beautifully carved logboats. Hollowed from kauri pine trees, they were up to 22 m (70 ft) long.

One-handed adze for fine hollowing

Wooden peg to fix plank extension to log base

Small mallet for driving in wooden pegs

DIGGING OUT
The outside of this Indonesian logboat has been roughly shaped and work has begun on hollowing it out. The depth of the boat is being increased by fitting a plank to the top edge of the hull. When the boat has taken shape, the hull will be rubbed down with fish skins, which work like sandpaper to give it a smooth finish.

COLOURFUL CARGO CARRIER
In Africa and South and Central America, logboats are still an important means of water transport. Fitted with a rudder and a spritsail or two (p. 24), dugouts like this carry goods around the sheltered waters of Cartagena harbour in Columbia. Very similar craft are found in Panama, where they are used for fishing.

Ring to which mooring rope or "painter" is tied

PACIFIC CANOE

This graceful fishing boat from the Solomon Islands is a very simple logboat. By adding a plank to its top edge and attaching an outrigger, it is possible to make a sailing-boat that can cross hundreds of kilometres of open sea. It was in such boats that explorers from Asia colonised the many thousands of islands that dot the vast Pacific Ocean.

Wooden "double U" connectives that join boom to float

Outrigger float

DO NOT DIG THIS TREE

Though they are abundant in Asia and the Pacific, palm trees and banana trees (right) are too narrow to make logboats. However, coir, coconut fibre, is spun to make rope to lash on boats (p. 16), and the leaves of both trees can be matted to make sails.

SAILING BACKWARDS

Like all outriggers, this *oruwa* from Sri Lanka has no fixed bow or stern. To change direction, the crew drops the sail and resets it at the other end of the boat.

LATE ARRIVALS

This Spanish galleon is arriving in the Pacific island of Guam in 1590. By that time Europeans were exploring and trading farther and farther eastwards. But it would take them another 200 years to discover some islands colonised many centuries earlier by sailors from Asia in dugout canoes.

Outrigger boom

OUTRIGGER CANOE

This outrigger canoe from Tonga is typical of craft found all over the Pacific. A shaped log or "float" has been attached to the narrow dugout hull to make it stable under sail. The float is always kept to windward, the side the wind is blowing from, where it acts as a counterbalance to the pressure of the wind on the sail. This stops the hull from blowing over.

Dugout hull

Boom lashed to hull through holes drilled in logboat

LOW-FLYING FISH

Pacific islanders catch a lot of flying fish, not just with their nets and hooks, but occasionally in their sails!

Thwart (seat)

Thwart with hole for mast

Ring for painter

Plank boats

BY FIXING A NUMBER of timbers together, it is possible to build a boat of virtually any shape. Such a "plank boat" can be very long and deep, unlike a logboat, which can only be as long as the tree it is made from. It can thus carry lots of passengers or cargo and sail safely in rough waters. Often the planks are fastened to a skeleton of sturdy pieces of wood, frames. Alternatively, timbers (ribs) may be inserted after the planks have been fastened together. A few plank boats have no frames or ribs at all. But most fall into one of two groups: edge-joined, where the planks are fastened edge to edge to form a smooth hull, or lapstrake, where each plank overlaps the one below it.

FLEXIBLE FERRY
Before the building of the harbour of Madras in southeast India, local boats had to brave heavy surf to ferry passengers and cargo to ships anchored offshore. Instead of being nailed, their planks were sewn together, to allow them to move as they were buffeted by the waves.

SEWING BOATS
The fishermen of India's east coast still sew their boats. They place a wad of coconut fibre (coir) or marsh grass between the drilled planks before lacing them together with coir rope.

One-piece frame (rib)

Plank joints coated with resin

Rattan (palm frond) lashing

Lugs

CARVED BOAT
Usually planks are cut straight and then heated and twisted into shape. But each plank of the *tora*, a canoe from the Solomon Islands, has been carved in a precise shape. Rattan – palm fronds – are used to sew the planks together. The ribs are then lashed to lugs, wooden projections left standing on each plank.

Hand-carved thwart (seat)

Bow sheathed with metal

BEASTLY CREW
The Bible says that Noah's Ark, the vessel that saved the animals from the Flood, was 133 m (430 ft) long. In this 13th-century English stained-glass window, it is shown as a hulc, a Northern European planked ship.

Square stern

NOSE IN THE AIR
This edge-joined Portuguese fishing boat is launched from a beach. It has a flat bottom that slides easily over the sand and a high prow that will never nosedive in rough surf. The square stern is formed by bottom planks which have been curved up sharply. This is a very skilled piece of work – most boats with square sterns are simply fitted with a large board, called the transom.

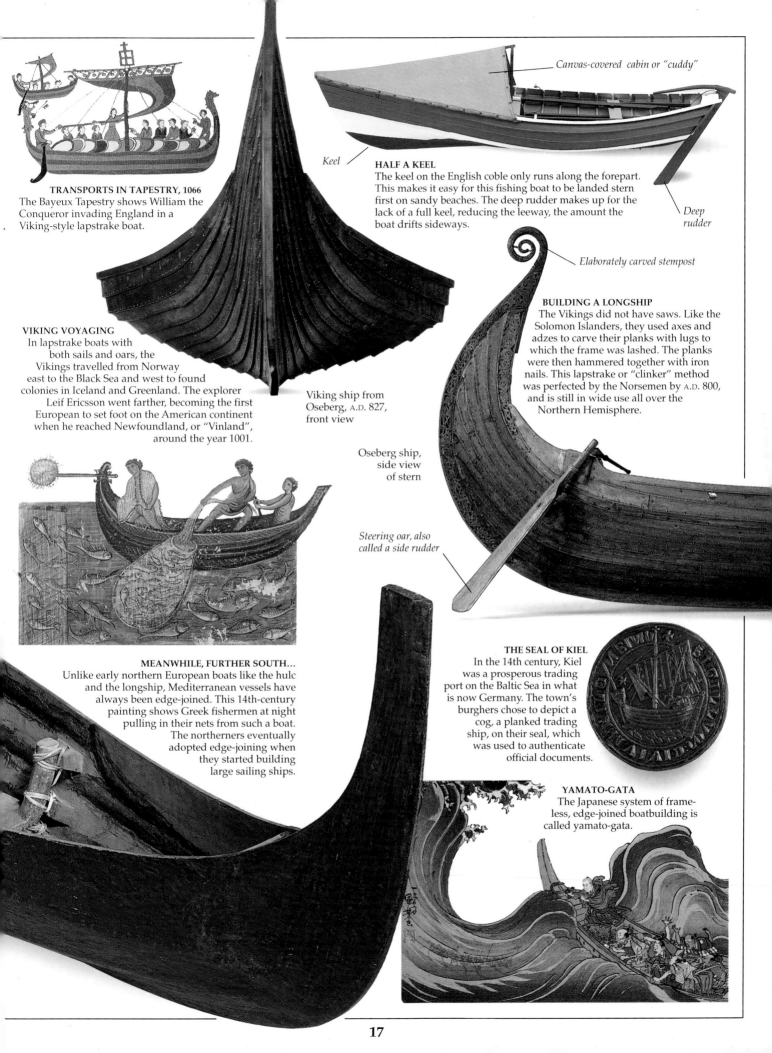

TRANSPORTS IN TAPESTRY, 1066
The Bayeux Tapestry shows William the Conqueror invading England in a Viking-style lapstrake boat.

Keel

HALF A KEEL
The keel on the English coble only runs along the forepart. This makes it easy for this fishing boat to be landed stern first on sandy beaches. The deep rudder makes up for the lack of a full keel, reducing the leeway, the amount the boat drifts sideways.

Canvas-covered cabin or "cuddy"

Deep rudder

Elaborately carved stempost

VIKING VOYAGING
In lapstrake boats with both sails and oars, the Vikings travelled from Norway east to the Black Sea and west to found colonies in Iceland and Greenland. The explorer Leif Ericsson went farther, becoming the first European to set foot on the American continent when he reached Newfoundland, or "Vinland", around the year 1001.

Viking ship from Oseberg, A.D. 827, front view

BUILDING A LONGSHIP
The Vikings did not have saws. Like the Solomon Islanders, they used axes and adzes to carve their planks with lugs to which the frame was lashed. The planks were then hammered together with iron nails. This lapstrake or "clinker" method was perfected by the Norsemen by A.D. 800, and is still in wide use all over the Northern Hemisphere.

Oseberg ship, side view of stern

Steering oar, also called a side rudder

MEANWHILE, FURTHER SOUTH...
Unlike early northern European boats like the hulc and the longship, Mediterranean vessels have always been edge-joined. This 14th-century painting shows Greek fishermen at night pulling in their nets from such a boat. The northerners eventually adopted edge-joining when they started building large sailing ships.

THE SEAL OF KIEL
In the 14th century, Kiel was a prosperous trading port on the Baltic Sea in what is now Germany. The town's burghers chose to depict a cog, a planked trading ship, on their seal, which was used to authenticate official documents.

YAMATO-GATA
The Japanese system of frameless, edge-joined boatbuilding is called yamato-gata.

Putting planks together

ALL PLANK BOATS ARE CONSTRUCTED from a number of flat pieces of wood, each cut to a particular shape. The planks are then twisted and fastened together by their edges. Many wooden boats (and all wooden ships) are built by first erecting a framework and then nailing on the planks. This "inside-out" method is known as skeleton construction. Some small craft are built the other way around, from the outside in. This is called shell construction. With this method a template or mould is used to fix the shape of the shell, which is then stiffened with an internal framework. The boat examined here is a small lapstrake craft (p. 16) constructed by the shell method with the help of wooden moulds.

PLANK MAKING
Until recently, planks had to be cut from logs and boards by hand, with a large saw wielded by two people. Nowadays, they are cut by machines.

Shore

Transom

Spall to hold boat to ceiling

Clamp to hold staves in position

Mallet for driving in wedges

Wedge

Wooden chain for copying curves in boat

Rib, not yet fully fixed

Shore to hold mould in place

Mould – as boat is symmetrical, only one half is needed

Centreline

Mould

BOATBUILDER'S SHED
This boat's stempost and transom (p. 16) are being held in position by spalls, wooden struts fastened to the ceiling. The planks on the starboard (right) side have been clamped in position. On the port (left) side, moulds are in place for planking up (adding more planks). Once this is complete, one-piece frames – ribs – will be fastened across the boat.

BOX PLANE
The plane is used to give angled edges to the planks, so that when they are fastened to each other, there is as much contact as possible.

Ball end for flattening nail ends

Small box plane

Copper nails

Marking scribe for scoring parallel edges

RIVETING STUFF
To fasten (or rivet) two overlapping planks together, holes are drilled through the overlap and nails driven in from the outside. Metal washers – roves – are then driven over the nail points with a roving punch and hammer. Finally, the sharp end is snapped off with pliers and flattened out with the hammer.

Copper roves

Ball pein hammer

Cutting pliers for snapping off nail ends

Roving punch

JIGSAW PUZZLE
A strake is a line of one or more planks which runs from one end of a boat to the other. These nine oddly shaped strakes make up one side of the boat below. Only one edge of all nine strakes is straight – the lower edge of the garboard, the strake which is fastened to the keel. After they are cut, the strakes will be put in a steam-filled box. Made soft and flexible, they are then bent around the moulds and fastened one on top of the other.

Top or "sheer" strake

Bottom or "garboard" strake

Spall

Apron, a timber added to strengthen bow

Sheer strake

Keel

Stempost

Garboard strake

Stempost

Strongback which supports keel in shed

Sheer strake

Rib

Toe cleat for rowing crutch

Thwart

Stringer, a horizontal strengthener

Transom

Keel

Oarsome power

HUMAN MUSCLE POWER is the most obvious and reliable way of driving a boat through the water. Small vessels can be punted (p. 6) or paddled, using a paddle held in both hands. Bigger boats may be rowed, with the help of an oar which pivots on the side of the boat. Paddles are far more manoeuvrable, but they are not as efficient, because rowing involves more muscles. The best way to row is to pull on the oar. But to do this you have to sit with your back to the bow, so you can't see where you are going! The ancient Greeks and Romans built huge oared warships known as galleys which were rowed by as many as 1,800 oarsmen. The slaves or prisoners who pulled the oars lived in appalling conditions. Galleys were still being used early in the 19th century.

TIED TO THE MAST
This Roman mosaic tells the legend of how the Greek hero Odysseus eluded the Sirens, sea creatures who sang beautifully to lure sailors onto the rocks. He made his crew block their ears with wax, though he was too curious to do the same. Then he had himself tied to the mast, so he would not leap overboard when he heard the singing.

Lateen sail for long distance travel, furled (rolled up) during battles

Fighting platform

Decorative ram

Bronze cannon

Ram

Square sail

Steering oar

Decorated oar blades, each pulled by three men

HARD-NOSED WARSHIP
Greek galleys were floating battering rams. When an enemy ship was spotted, the galley would be rowed into it at full speed, to try to hole and sink it with the ram, the long projection on the bow. This vase from 510 B.C. shows a small galley with only one bank of oars. The Greeks also built larger "biremes" with two banks of oars and "triremes" powered by three banks.

Blade, the surface that pushes against the water

Steering oar from a Fijian *proa*, a sailing boat with an outrigger

GOOD BLADES
The blade of the racing oar is shaped like a spoon, to give it maximum push. The gondolier twists his oar in the water, so he never has to lift it out as he rows. The Fijian steering oar acts like a rudder. It is not known why the *umla* oar has such an odd shape.

TWO HANDED
His face towards the bow of the boat, this Malaysian boy is sculling – rowing with one oar in each hand. He is doing so with crossed oars, a method only found in Southeast Asia.

Racing oar

Oar from Portuguese river boat

Venetian gondolier's oar

Oar from an *umla*, a large Arabian fishing boat

Steering oar

Pennant decorated with fleur-de-lis

BANGING THE DRUM
Films and cartoons often show a Roman drummer who kept time for the oarsmen. In fact, this job was usually done by a musician playing the flute!

STATELY DOWN THE INDUS
This Indian barge was still being used by the Maharajah of Udaipur in the 1930s. It was unusual because the Indian prince sat high in the bow, looking back at his oarsmen. Both paddles and oars can be used for steering. In this case, the barge is guided with a single oar over the port quarter.

Bow

FRENCH STYLE
Built in the late 17th century, this French galley was propelled by 60 oars and two lateen sails (p. 25). Galleys were popular with Algerian pirates, and the French copied some of their craft. Like the Greek galley, this one has a ram. A few galleys were merchant vessels, but most were warships. The last battle between galleys was fought at Lepanto in the eastern Mediterranean in 1571. But because they were very fast over short distances, the French navy still had war galleys at the beginning of the 19th century.

Paddle from a *yabiduna* New Guinean outrigger

Coracle paddle

Double-bladed plastic kayak paddle

Zaire dugout paddle

Paddle from a *caballito*, a Peruvian reed boat

PADDLE POWER
To stop a canoe from going around in circles, these paddles from New Guinea and Zaire must be dipped into the water on both sides of the canoe. The kayak and caballito paddles are double-bladed, which makes this operation easy. The coracle paddle is swept over the bow, pulling the boat along.

Blowing in the wind

THE ENERGY OF MOVING AIR can push a boat through the water. This is sailing, and people have been doing it for almost as long as they have been making boats. The first sail was probably a hand-held cloth. The next step was to attach it to a mast. This is kept upright by the standing rigging, consisting of shrouds which stop the mast from moving sideways and stays which stop it falling forwards or backwards. The sail itself may be hung from a stay. But usually it hangs from a pole or spar called a yard and is supported at the bottom by another spar, the boom. The sails are controlled by ropes called sheets, which are continually adjusted to keep the sails roughly at right angles to the wind.

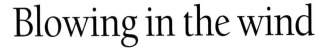

RUNNING WITH THE WIND
How close a boat can sail towards the wind depends on the type of sails it has. But for every boat there is a "no-go zone". The various directions a boat can take in relation to the wind are called the points of sailing. Reaching, for instance, is sailing across the wind.

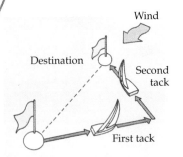

Trapeze wire, which runs between top of mast and harness

TACKY ZIGZAGS
Because it cannot sail straight into the wind, a boat must cut a zig-zag course when it heads upwind. This called tacking. Turning when the wind is behind the boat is known as gybing.

TRAPEZE ARTIST
To counteract the push of the wind and keep the boat as upright as possible, the helmsman and his crew are leaning out of the windward side of the boat. The crew is standing on the edge of the boat and hanging far out on a trapeze, a harness attached to a wire running to the top of the mast.

Tiller extension

Main sheet

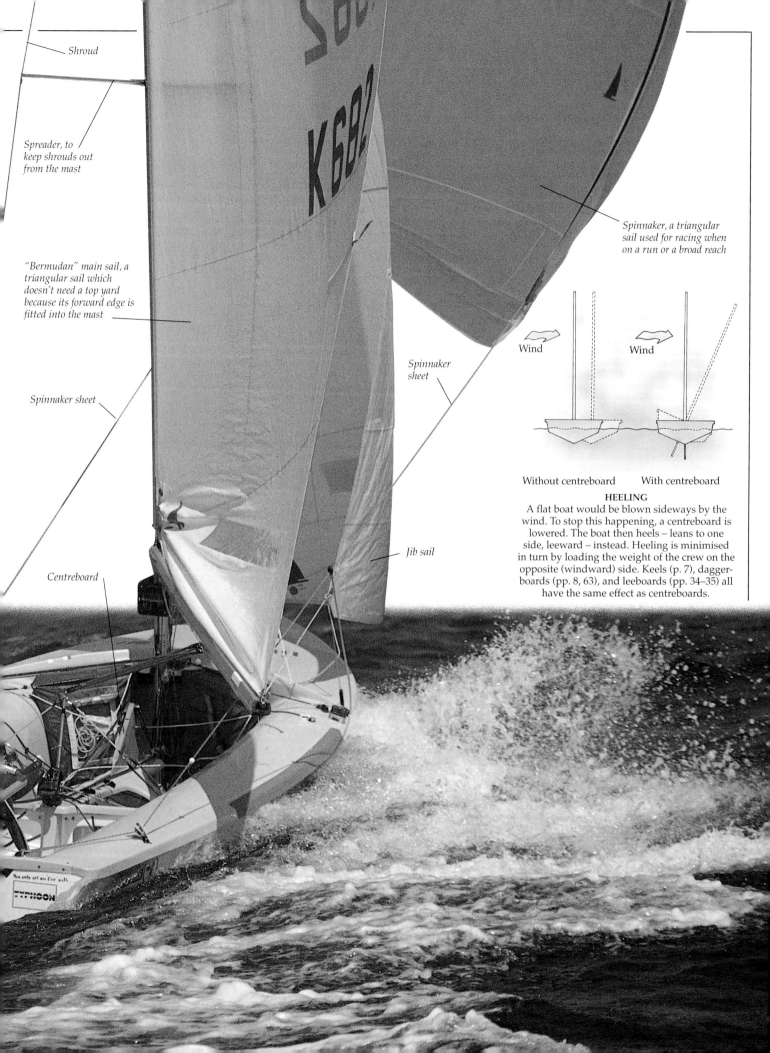

Shroud

Spreader, to keep shrouds out from the mast

"Bermudan" main sail, a triangular sail which doesn't need a top yard because its forward edge is fitted into the mast

Spinnaker sheet

Centreboard

Spinnaker, a triangular sail used for racing when on a run or a broad reach

Spinnaker sheet

Jib sail

Wind

Wind

Without centreboard

With centreboard

HEELING
A flat boat would be blown sideways by the wind. To stop this happening, a centreboard is lowered. The boat then heels – leans to one side, leeward – instead. Heeling is minimised in turn by loading the weight of the crew on the opposite (windward) side. Keels (p. 7), dagger-boards (pp. 8, 63), and leeboards (pp. 34–35) all have the same effect as centreboards.

Sail style

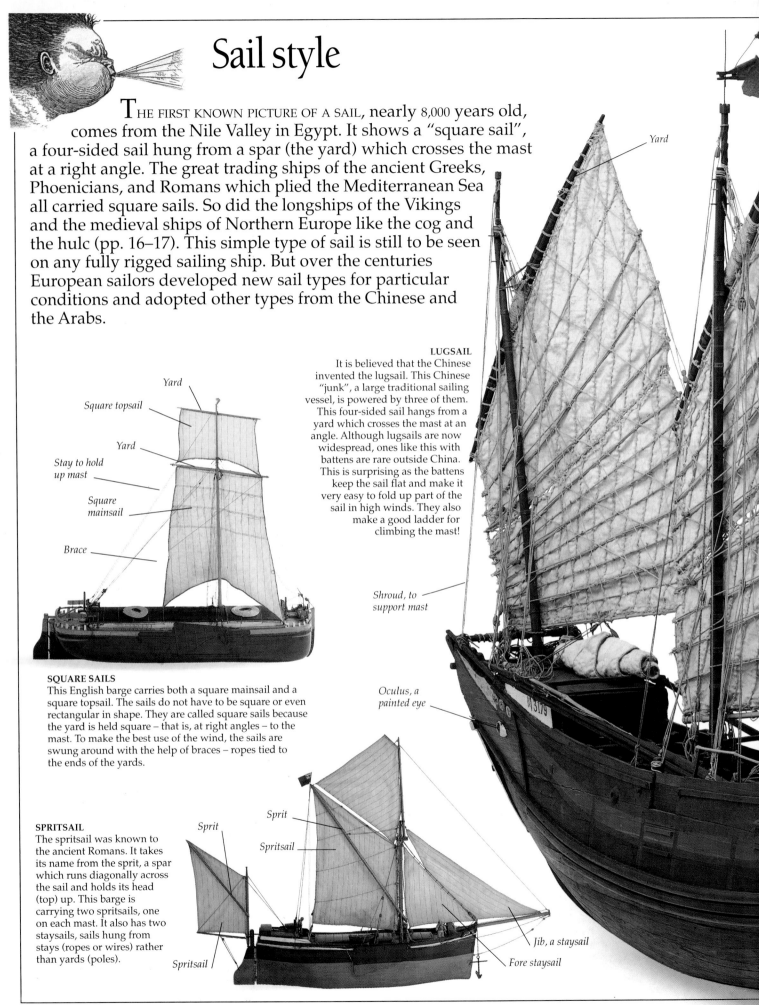

The first known picture of a sail, nearly 8,000 years old, comes from the Nile Valley in Egypt. It shows a "square sail", a four-sided sail hung from a spar (the yard) which crosses the mast at a right angle. The great trading ships of the ancient Greeks, Phoenicians, and Romans which plied the Mediterranean Sea all carried square sails. So did the longships of the Vikings and the medieval ships of Northern Europe like the cog and the hulc (pp. 16–17). This simple type of sail is still to be seen on any fully rigged sailing ship. But over the centuries European sailors developed new sail types for particular conditions and adopted other types from the Chinese and the Arabs.

LUGSAIL
It is believed that the Chinese invented the lugsail. This Chinese "junk", a large traditional sailing vessel, is powered by three of them. This four-sided sail hangs from a yard which crosses the mast at an angle. Although lugsails are now widespread, ones like this with battens are rare outside China. This is surprising as the battens keep the sail flat and make it very easy to fold up part of the sail in high winds. They also make a good ladder for climbing the mast!

Yard

Shroud, to support mast

Oculus, a painted eye

Yard

Square topsail

Yard

Stay to hold up mast

Square mainsail

Brace

SQUARE SAILS
This English barge carries both a square mainsail and a square topsail. The sails do not have to be square or even rectangular in shape. They are called square sails because the yard is held square – that is, at right angles – to the mast. To make the best use of the wind, the sails are swung around with the help of braces – ropes tied to the ends of the yards.

SPRITSAIL
The spritsail was known to the ancient Romans. It takes its name from the sprit, a spar which runs diagonally across the sail and holds its head (top) up. This barge is carrying two spritsails, one on each mast. It also has two staysails, sails hung from stays (ropes or wires) rather than yards (poles).

Sprit

Sprit

Spritsail

Spritsail

Jib, a staysail

Fore staysail

SETTEE
The settee is a triangular sail on which the leading corner of the foot (bottom) has been cut off square. It is most often seen on Arab trading vessels called dhows, though this example is on a fishing boat on the River Nile.

Yard

Lateen sail

Lateen sail

Kuwaiti flag

LATEEN
This pearling dhow from Kuwait carries two triangular or "lateen" sails. Like the lugsail, the lateen is known as a fore-and-aft sail because its yard runs along the boat (that is, from fore to aft) rather than across it. Probably developed by Arab sailors, it was the forerunner of the settee. It is quite a cumbersome sail. When sailors go about (turn), they have to slacken the rigging and swing the yard to the other side of the mast.

Yard

Bamboo batten, to keep sail stiff

Mizzen mast

OCEANIC LATEEN
The triangular sail on this Indonesian boat from Bali is another lateen. It is set from a very short mast, hidden in the picture by the billowing sail.

Mizzen mast

Lateen sail

Mainmast

Foremast

Square topsail

Sampan tender

Ropes to raise rudder in port and lower it in deep water

Bowsprit

MIXED SAILS
Known as a caravel, this 15th-century Portuguese ship carried square sails on her bowsprit and front mast (the foremast) but lateen sails on her other three masts. Two centuries later, fully rigged ships had square sails on all three masts with a lateen only on the third mast (the mizzen).

The Age of Sail

L IKE SPACESHIPS, SAILING SHIPS travelled to new worlds. In the 15th century, they took Christopher Columbus to America and Vasco de Gama around Africa to India. Three hundred years later a sailing ship took James Cook to the South Seas and on to Australia. Thanks to the sailing ship, the continents and oceans were explored and charted. In the wake of the explorers came trading ships carrying the exotic spices, textiles, tobacco, and other products of the Orient and the Americas to Europe. Across the centuries, sailing the seven seas was a way of life for many men (and the occasional woman). There were always decks to caulk, yards to brace, watches to keep, and sails to reef, furl, and mend. And ever present was the sea, always unpredictable and capable of rising in the sudden fury of a storm.

DOWN THE SLIPPERY SLOPE
Launching a ship is a fine art (pp. 46–47). This 18th-century bowl shows a brig (p. 27) on the slipway. Men with hammers stand poised, waiting for the signal to knock away the wooden supports. The ship will then slide slowly, stern first, down a greased slope into the water. Only then will her masts be raised and rigged (equipped with ropes and sails).

Fid, for making large holes in canvas

Seam rubber

Needles

Pricker, for making small holes in canvas

Hole for thumb

Bullock's horn filled with wax for holding neeedles

Thimbles, sewn into edges of sail. Ropes can then be tied to thimbles

Punch set for making thimbles

Twine

Sailmaker's palm

TOOLS OF THE SAILMAKER
Until recently, sails were made by hand by sewing strips of heavy canvas together. Every large ship had a sailmaker in its crew, as sails were often damaged and had to be mended at sea. The sailmaker's tools included a "rubber", used to make sharp creases in the canvas before sewing, and a palm, to protect the hand from the needle as it was pushed through the canvas.

IN THE SAILMAKER'S LOFT
This sailmaker is finishing a seam, while another sail is being stretched. Both sails will be finished by sewing a rope all the way around their edges.

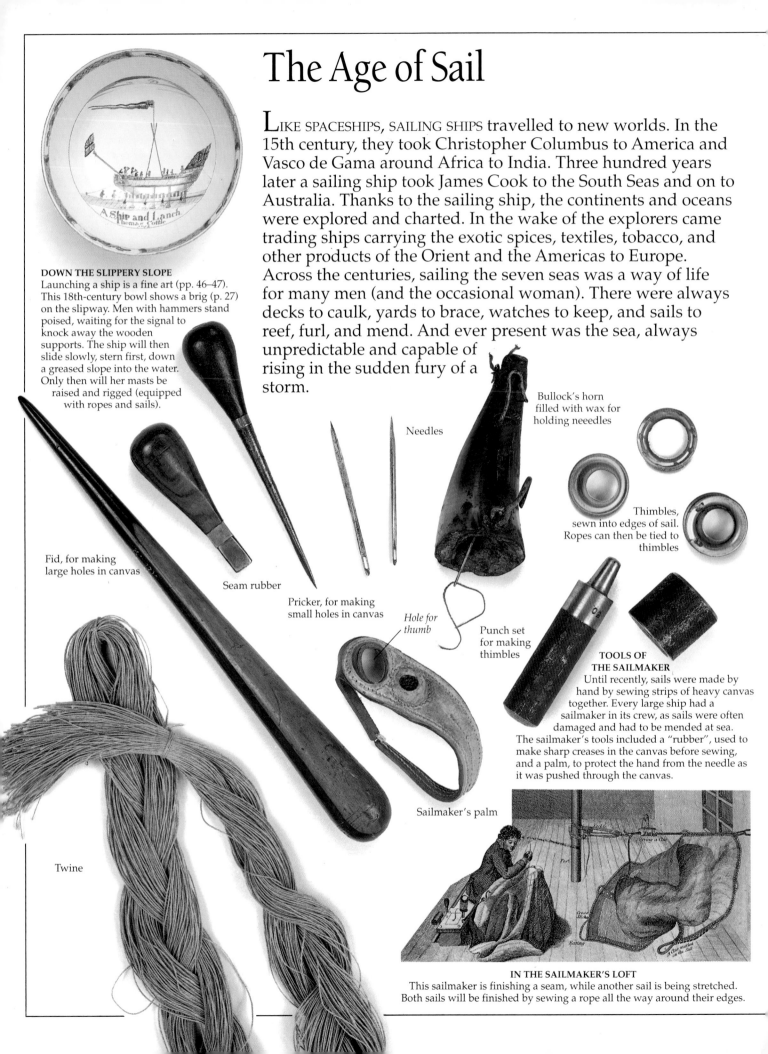

Foremast

Main mast

Fore royal

Main royal

Fore topgallant

Main topgallant
studding sails

POOPED
Caught in a storm, this ship
(the *Joseph Sampson*) is in danger
of being pooped. Pooping happens
when a wave breaks over the stern.
This may cause the ship to veer
wildly off course. If she turns
across the waves, she may
well capsize.

Fore topsail

Flying jib

Outer jib

Inner jib

Bowsprit

Gaff sail

Lower
studding sail

Dolphin striker, for
holding down bowsprit

Boom for
studding sail

Figurehead

Fore staysail

Foresail

FULL SAIL AHEAD
This is a merchant ship of the mid-19th century.
Because she has two masts both rigged with square sails, she is
technically known as a brig. She is sailing with a light wind behind
her, and her crew has set as many sails as they can. From the ends
of the main, top, and topgallant yards, short yards and booms
have been run out to set extra sails. These "studding sails" were
carried by all sailing ships from early in the 18th century.

KEEPING THE WATER OUT
The caulker keeps a ship's planks
watertight, by driving old rope
into the seams between them
and then sealing them up
with tar.

SEA GROWTH
This bottle was
pulled from the sea
encrusted with
barnacles. These sticky
crustaceans also attach
themselves to the hulls of
wooden ships, slowing the
vessels down.

SHIP WORM
Worms like the
teredo bore holes
into the wooden hulls of
sailing ships. By the late
17th century, many ships were
sheathed with copper plates
to keep the destructive
molluscs out.

Continued on next page

Continued from previous page

SHOW A LEG
The hammock was adopted from the natives of the West Indies in the 16th century. Before then, sailors slept on the deck.

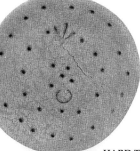

SAILOR'S FAREWELL
The sailor saying goodbye to his sweetheart was a popular theme for 18th-century artists.

Sailing for a living

In ships laden with tea from China, manufactured goods from Europe, and sugar from the West Indies, sailors spent many months away from home. They lived in cramped and filthy conditions and had to be tough. Their diet was poor – after the first few days at sea there would be no more fresh vegetables or fruit. For all this, sailors were poorly paid. A few became pirates, making a more profitable living by stealing the cargoes of other ships.

OFF DUTY
These men are relaxing over a meal at the mess table of a sailing warship. The gunports are open to let in air and light. In a battle, the gun deck is cleared away and the men busy themselves rapidly loading and firing the cannon.

HARD TACK
Sailors in the British Navy were issued with ¹/₂ kg (1 lb) of these rock-hard biscuits every day.

SUGAR ISLAND
This 17th-century map of Barbados shows a sugar mill worked by slaves. Sugar plantations in the West Indies made vast fortunes for their owners.

PREVENTATIVE MEDICINE
To stop getting the disease scurvy, which is caused by a lack of Vitamin C, British sailors ate limes. This made American sailors nickname them "Limeys".

FELLOW TRAVELLER
The holds of most ships were infested with rats. Fleas that lived on the rats carried the plague from country to country.

BARBADOS WATERS
These measuring jugs and 27-litre (6-gallon) breaker are for issuing daily rations of "Barbados waters" – rum – to British sailors. Rum is distilled from sugar cane and was favoured on board ship because it kept much longer than beer. Common sailors were given grog, a mixture of four parts water to one part rum.

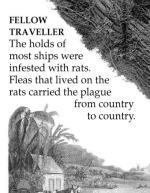

ROLL OUT THE BARREL
On the West Indian island of Antigua, barrels of sugar are loaded onto a boat which will then carry them to the trading ship anchored offshore. In a few weeks, the sugar will be on sale in Europe.

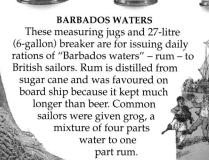

PORT OF CALL
This is Portsmouth in England at the beginning of the 19th century. Like all ports, it had a lively and sometimes violent area where sailors could enjoy themselves and spend their savings.

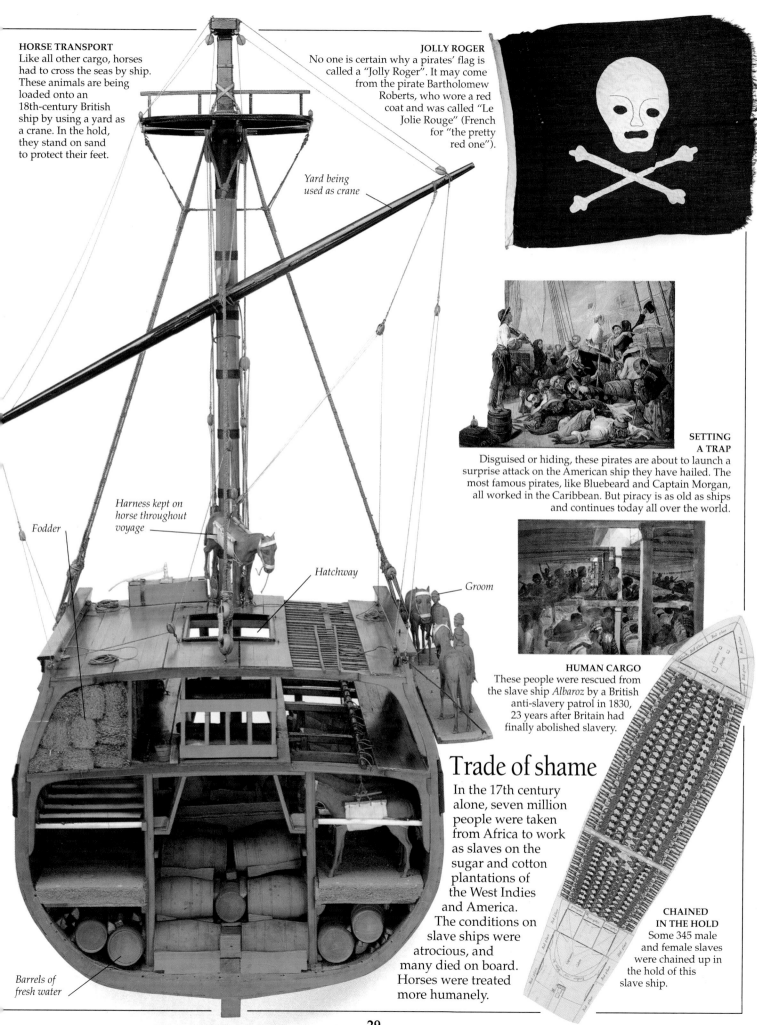

HORSE TRANSPORT
Like all other cargo, horses had to cross the seas by ship. These animals are being loaded onto an 18th-century British ship by using a yard as a crane. In the hold, they stand on sand to protect their feet.

JOLLY ROGER
No one is certain why a pirates' flag is called a "Jolly Roger". It may come from the pirate Bartholomew Roberts, who wore a red coat and was called "Le Jolie Rouge" (French for "the pretty red one").

Yard being used as crane

Harness kept on horse throughout voyage

Fodder

Hatchway

Groom

Barrels of fresh water

SETTING A TRAP
Disguised or hiding, these pirates are about to launch a surprise attack on the American ship they have hailed. The most famous pirates, like Bluebeard and Captain Morgan, all worked in the Caribbean. But piracy is as old as ships and continues today all over the world.

HUMAN CARGO
These people were rescued from the slave ship *Albaroz* by a British anti-slavery patrol in 1830, 23 years after Britain had finally abolished slavery.

Trade of shame

In the 17th century alone, seven million people were taken from Africa to work as slaves on the sugar and cotton plantations of the West Indies and America. The conditions on slave ships were atrocious, and many died on board. Horses were treated more humanely.

CHAINED IN THE HOLD
Some 345 male and female slaves were chained up in the hold of this slave ship.

Thar' she blows!

WHEN HE SPIED a column of water vapour rising from the sea, the look-out on board a whaling ship raised the alarm with the traditional cry of "Thar' she blows!" Small boats were launched and rowed out to harpoon the whale, which had given away its presence by coming to the surface and breathing out. For hundreds of years, local hunters all over the world have launched boats from the beach to chase whales for meat. But in the heyday of whaling in the early 19th century, American and European whalers (whaling ships) undertook long voyages around the world in pursuit of these ocean giants. The cruel and bloody hunt kept the world light and clean, for whale oil was burnt in lamps and used to make soap and cosmetics. With the discovery of a more abundant oil – petroleum – in the 1860s, the demand for whales declined. But despite strong protests, whaling for meat continues in several countries to this day.

Sail of matted palm leaves

Harpoon

Paddle

INDONESIAN WHALER
The people of Lamalera on the Indonesian island of Lembata hunt sperm whales from boats like this. Like 19th-century European whalers, they use hand-thrown harpoons to catch the whales, which are often two to three times longer than the boats that hunt them.

WOODEN WHALE
Carved by a sailor on a long voyage, this wooden model of a sperm whale is inlaid with a harpoon of bone. The sperm whale's huge square head is full of a liquid wax called spermaceti, which was used to make candles and cosmetics. The right whale and the sperm whale were the most commercially important. But all ten species of great whale (including the largest animal ever to have lived, the blue whale) have been hunted, some almost to the point of extinction.

TOOLS OF THE TRADE
The boathook is a general tool used to bring anything – be it a rope or a whale – towards the boat. These sharp harpoons, hurled into the surfacing whale, have pivoting barbs on their heads, to keep them firmly lodged in the beast's flesh. The lance was not thrown but stabbed into the whale. The broad boatspade was used to cut out a hole in the whale's tail through which a towing rope could then be tied.

Harpoon

Spare harpoon

Boathook

Lance

Line

Boatspade

HARPOONING
The whale would dive when struck by the harpoon, which was tied to a very long line of rope. The whaleboat would then be towed through the water until the whale surfaced to breathe and dived again. This could go on for hours. When the exhausted leviathan finally surfaced for the last time, the boat would close in and the bowman would kill it by driving a lance into its underbelly.

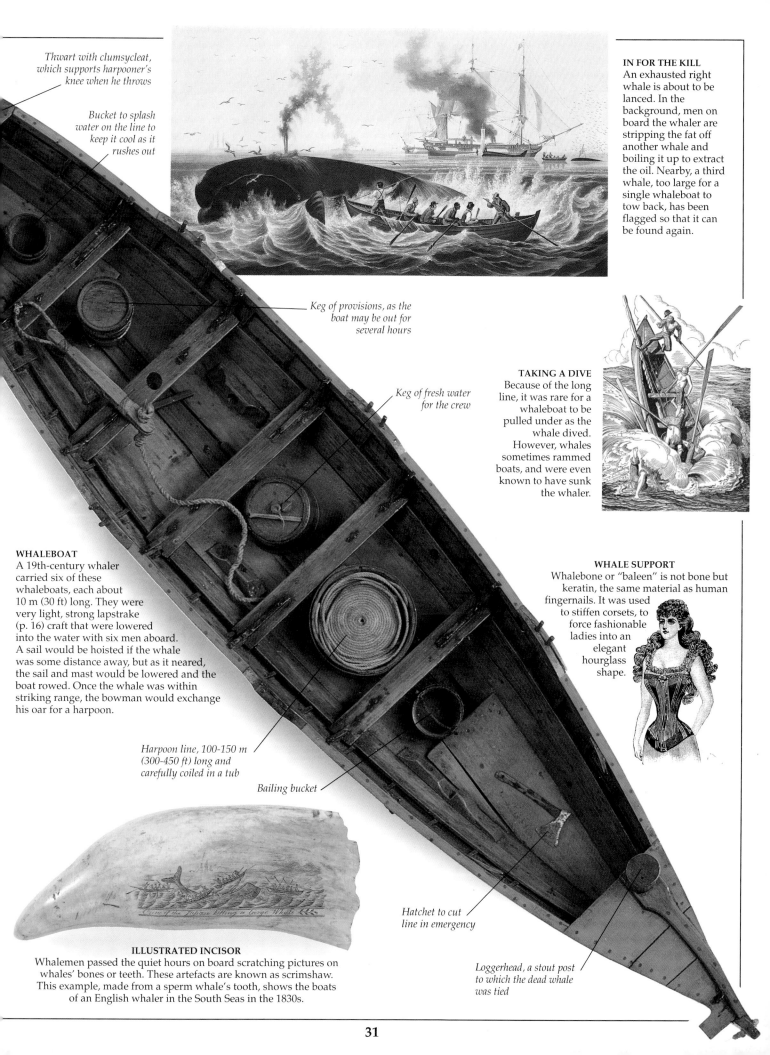

Thwart with clumsycleat, which supports harpooner's knee when he throws

Bucket to splash water on the line to keep it cool as it rushes out

(p. 16)

IN FOR THE KILL
An exhausted right whale is about to be lanced. In the background, men on board the whaler are stripping the fat off another whale and boiling it up to extract the oil. Nearby, a third whale, too large for a single whaleboat to tow back, has been flagged so that it can be found again.

Keg of provisions, as the boat may be out for several hours

Keg of fresh water for the crew

TAKING A DIVE
Because of the long line, it was rare for a whaleboat to be pulled under as the whale dived. However, whales sometimes rammed boats, and were even known to have sunk the whaler.

WHALEBOAT
A 19th-century whaler carried six of these whaleboats, each about 10 m (30 ft) long. They were very light, strong lapstrake (p. 16) craft that were lowered into the water with six men aboard. A sail would be hoisted if the whale was some distance away, but as it neared, the sail and mast would be lowered and the boat rowed. Once the whale was within striking range, the bowman would exchange his oar for a harpoon.

WHALE SUPPORT
Whalebone or "baleen" is not bone but keratin, the same material as human fingernails. It was used to stiffen corsets, to force fashionable ladies into an elegant hourglass shape.

Harpoon line, 100-150 m (300-450 ft) long and carefully coiled in a tub

Bailing bucket

Hatchet to cut line in emergency

ILLUSTRATED INCISOR
Whalemen passed the quiet hours on board scratching pictures on whales' bones or teeth. These artefacts are known as scrimshaw. This example, made from a sperm whale's tooth, shows the boats of an English whaler in the South Seas in the 1830s.

Loggerhead, a stout post to which the dead whale was tied

Polished steel

Painted wood

A splash of colour

Because their lives depend on them, people have strong affections for their boats. To make them more beautiful or individual, sailing boats and ships are often decorated with paintwork or elaborate carvings. Traditionally sailing ships had a carved or painted figure – the figurehead – on the bow, which often reflected the ship's name. In contrast, modern motor and steam ships are scarcely decorated at all.

VENETIAN STEEL
The steel bow of the gondola (p. 34) protects it and acts as a counterbalance to the weight of the gondolier at the stern. The six prongs symbolise the six wards into which Venice is divided.

ROMAN BIRD
Forged in the 1st century A.D., this bronze goosehead probably adorned the stern of a small Roman merchant ship.

DOGFISH HEAD
A fanciful creature – half dog, half fish – decorates the bow of this 18th-century barge made for the British royal family.

Winged figure of victory

Notch where boom sits

PRETTY PENNY
This coin shows the bow of a warship with an oculus. It commemorates the Cypriot victory in the sea battle of Salamis in 306 B.C.

Boom crutch for fishing boat from Surabaya in Indonesia

POLYNESIAN STYLE
A 15th-century Maori craftsman from the North Island of New Zealand carved this figure to adorn a canoe.

SALTY STERN
This colourful stern belongs to a very functional boat, a wooden *jangola* that carries salt between the Indonesian island of Madura and the mainland.

MYSTERIOUS PRESIDENT
This figurehead of Abraham Lincoln, President of the USA, was washed up on a beach in the Scilly Isles off the southwest coast of England. What ship it came from, how it sank, and what happened to its crew are all mysteries.

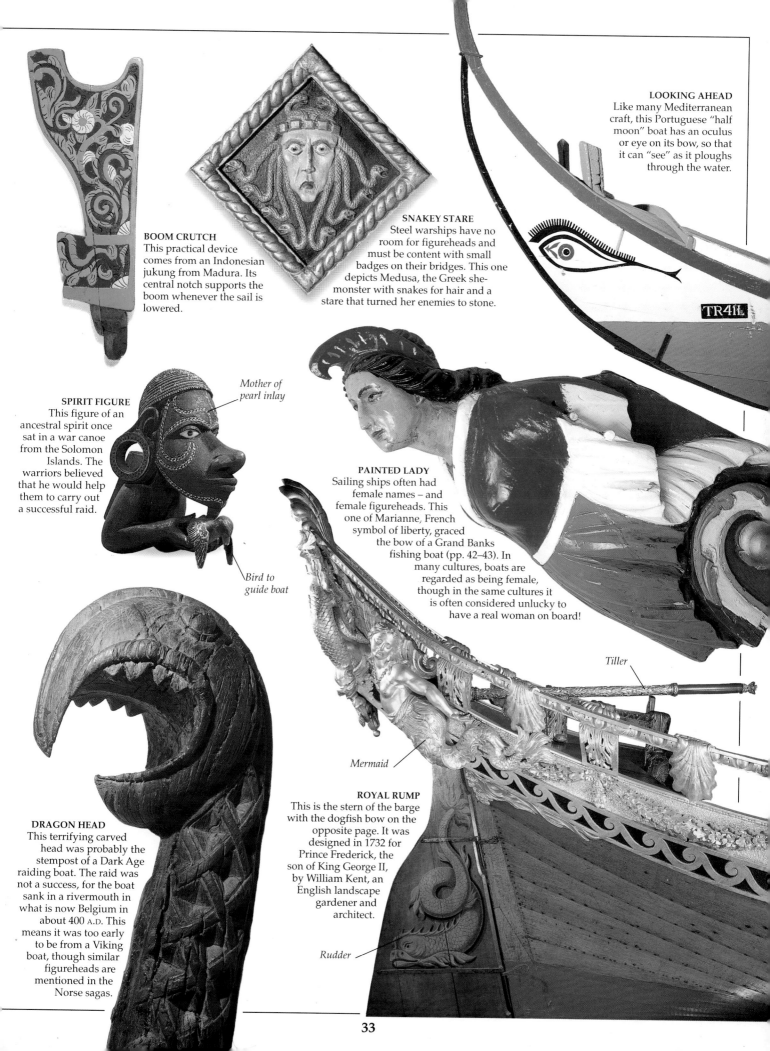

BOOM CRUTCH
This practical device comes from an Indonesian jukung from Madura. Its central notch supports the boom whenever the sail is lowered.

SNAKEY STARE
Steel warships have no room for figureheads and must be content with small badges on their bridges. This one depicts Medusa, the Greek she-monster with snakes for hair and a stare that turned her enemies to stone.

LOOKING AHEAD
Like many Mediterranean craft, this Portuguese "half moon" boat has an oculus or eye on its bow, so that it can "see" as it ploughs through the water.

TR41

SPIRIT FIGURE
This figure of an ancestral spirit once sat in a war canoe from the Solomon Islands. The warriors believed that he would help them to carry out a successful raid.

Mother of pearl inlay

Bird to guide boat

PAINTED LADY
Sailing ships often had female names – and female figureheads. This one of Marianne, French symbol of liberty, graced the bow of a Grand Banks fishing boat (pp. 42–43). In many cultures, boats are regarded as being female, though in the same cultures it is often considered unlucky to have a real woman on board!

Tiller

Mermaid

DRAGON HEAD
This terrifying carved head was probably the stempost of a Dark Age raiding boat. The raid was not a success, for the boat sank in a rivermouth in what is now Belgium in about 400 A.D. This means it was too early to be from a Viking boat, though similar figureheads are mentioned in the Norse sagas.

ROYAL RUMP
This is the stern of the barge with the dogfish bow on the opposite page. It was designed in 1732 for Prince Frederick, the son of King George II, by William Kent, an English landscape gardener and architect.

Rudder

In sheltered waters

Skewed stern

MOVING PEOPLE AND GOODS on water has always been cheaper than moving them about on land. Most countries have rivers, lakes, lagoons, and other natural waterways. Many nations have added to these by building extensive canal systems, along which cargo barges sail, steam, putt, or are towed. Great canals like the ones at Suez and Panama were dug to shorten the journeys of ocean-going ships. Special boats have been developed on all these inland waterways. Some are built to be highly manoeuvrable for work in confined spaces, like the asymmetrical gondola which ferries passengers along the narrow canals of Venice. Most are flat-bottomed, so they can run aground without getting stuck or toppling over. A flat bottom also gives a boat more cargo space, but the absence of a keel makes it hard to handle in rough waters. So some canal boats have leeboards, strong side-mounted stabilisers that make them more seaworthy.

CROOKED CONSTRUCTION
The gondola is fatter and wider on one side, the port side, than the other. This means the gondolier can row with one oar and still go in a straight line.

VENETIAN WATER TAXI
This gondola is ready for a wedding party. At one time rich families competed to have the most lavish gondolas, until the Venetian state decreed that they must all be black (p. 32).

HONG KONG HOUSEBOATS
On the incredibly crowded island of Hong Kong, many people make their homes on small, flat-bottomed boats called junks (pp. 24–25) or sampans.

GREEK SHIPPING LANE
Saltwater canals, like this one which cuts a channel between the Gulf of Corinth and the Saronic Gulf, are examples of making the water suit the ships, rather than making the ships suit the water!

ONE HORSE POWER
Towpaths were laid alongside the canals built in Britain in the 18th and into the 19th centuries, so that the narrow barges could be towed by horses.

FRESH FISH FERRY
A Chinese merchant uses this "sampan", Chinese for "three planks", to collect fish from fishermen all around Lake Donting. He loads the live fish into compartments in the hull and takes them to a market down the Yangtze River. The countless kilometres of rivers, lakes, and canals that cross China have given rise to hundreds of types of sampan.

Support for bad weather canopy

Sliding awning

Bamboo punt pole for pushing boat along

Open stern where two outboard motors are mounted

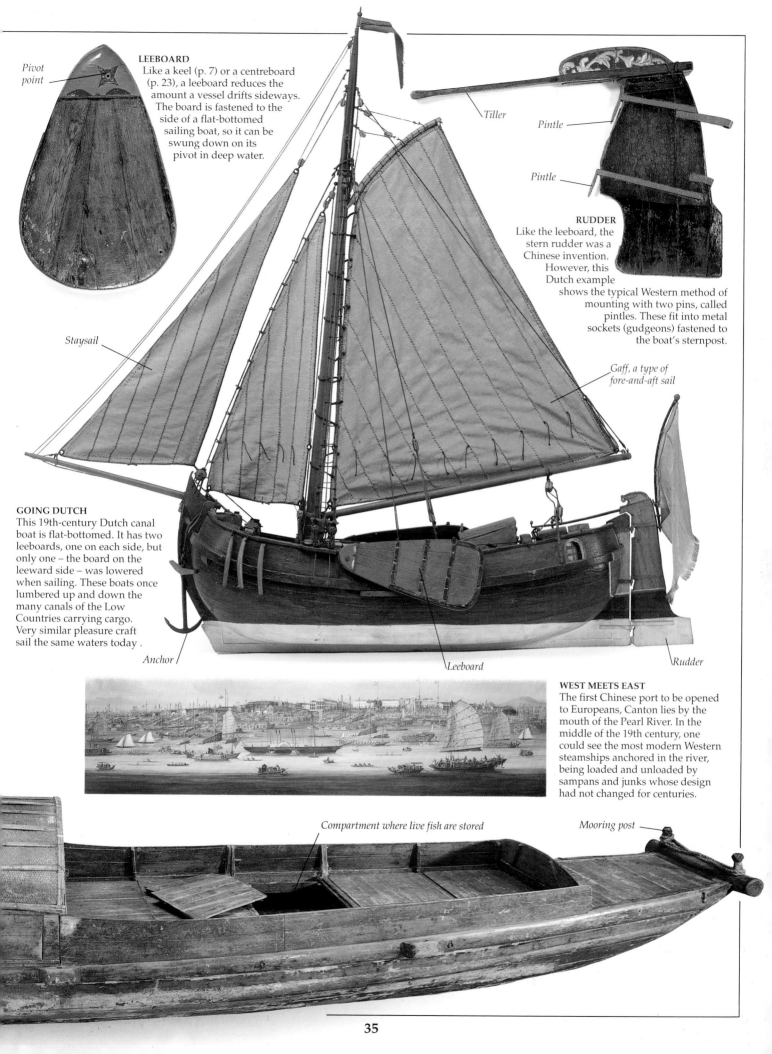

LEEBOARD

Pivot point

Like a keel (p. 7) or a centreboard (p. 23), a leeboard reduces the amount a vessel drifts sideways. The board is fastened to the side of a flat-bottomed sailing boat, so it can be swung down on its pivot in deep water.

Tiller

Pintle

Pintle

RUDDER

Like the leeboard, the stern rudder was a Chinese invention. However, this Dutch example shows the typical Western method of mounting with two pins, called pintles. These fit into metal sockets (gudgeons) fastened to the boat's sternpost.

Staysail

Gaff, a type of fore-and-aft sail

GOING DUTCH

This 19th-century Dutch canal boat is flat-bottomed. It has two leeboards, one on each side, but only one – the board on the leeward side – was lowered when sailing. These boats once lumbered up and down the many canals of the Low Countries carrying cargo. Very similar pleasure craft sail the same waters today.

Anchor

Leeboard

Rudder

WEST MEETS EAST

The first Chinese port to be opened to Europeans, Canton lies by the mouth of the Pearl River. In the middle of the 19th century, one could see the most modern Western steamships anchored in the river, being loaded and unloaded by sampans and junks whose design had not changed for centuries.

Compartment where live fish are stored

Mooring post

Steam and paddlewheels

As THE STEAM ENGINE was developed in the 18th century, inventors and engineers experimented with new mechanical ways of driving boats and ships. The first big development were paddlewheels. As these huge wheels turned, their flat blades dipped into the water and pushed a vessel along. Paddle steamers were very manoeuvrable, and were soon travelling all around the world. But they were particularly suited to the shallow waters of rivers and lakes. The most famous were the elegant paddle steamers of the Mississippi, which are still going strong – the world's largest river boat is the *Mississippi Queen*. However, for sea-going ships the propeller soon gained the upper hand.

UP A CREEK
Paddle steamers are too wide for narrow rivers. In *The African Queen*, film stars Humphrey Bogart and Katherine Hepburn had enough trouble navigating a small screw steamer in the rivers of East Africa.

PALATIAL FREIGHTERS
In their day, the Mississippi steamers were as luxurious as the great liners of a later age (pp. 54–57). But first and foremost they were cargo carriers, collecting produce and delivering supplies to 50 stops on the river between Memphis and New Orleans.

STERNWHEELER
Instead of two paddlewheels, one on each side, sternwheelers have a single wheel at the rear. They can work in shallower water than sidewheelers. This is a modern replica of the sternwheeler *Natchez*. In her first year, 1894, she made 50 trips between New Orleans and Vickersburg and carried over 56,000 bales of cotton.

STEAMER NATCHEZ
PORT OF NEW ORLEANS

Entrance to below deck accommodation

Paddle cover or "sponson"

CATCH A PACKET
The *King Alfred* was a packet steamer, a boat that carried passengers and goods on short, fixed routes.

Sponson

PUBLIC TRANSPORT, 1905
The *King Alfred* was one of 30 paddle steamers commissioned by London's council to ease the pressure on the city's busy roads and railways. But the service was not popular and was stopped two years later. The *King Alfred* went on to Germany where she made excursion trips on the Rhine and Elbe rivers until she was broken up (scrapped) in 1965.

STEAMING ACROSS THE ATLANTIC
In 1819, *Savannah* became the first steamer to cross the Atlantic, taking 21 days to travel from her home port in Georgia to Liverpool. However, she relied on her sails for most of the voyage. It was another 19 years before a British ship, *Sirius*, made the first crossing entirely under steam.

RECORD BREAKER
A cross-section of *Persia* shows her huge paddle-wheels, each 12 m (40 ft) in diameter. She was built in 1860 to be the fastest ship across the Atlantic, and went on to make several record-breaking runs.

Crankshaft

Paddle blade

Benches on deck

STEAMING UP
This is a 320 horse-power marine beam engine from the 1840s. A coal fire heats fresh water to generate steam. This travels along pipes to the cylinder where it forces a piston to move. The piston then moves the beam or crankshaft, which turns the paddle wheel.

Cylinder casing

Steam outlet

Piston rod

BEST OF BOTH WHIRLS
Launched in 1858, the *Great Eastern* (p. 47) was six times bigger than any ship yet made. She had both paddle wheels for shallow water and a screw propeller for speed in the open ocean.

Turn of the screw

IN 1845, A TUG-OF-WAR was held between a paddle steamer and a steamer powered by a propeller or "screw". The propeller proved to be the stronger of the two, pulling the paddle steamer backwards through the water. By that date many people were working on perfecting the propeller, including John Ericsson and Francis Pettit Smith. But the idea is a very old one. The ancient Greeks raised water with the help of Archimedes' screw, a device that looks like a corkscrew in a tube. As the screw turns, its thread pulls water up the tube. Some early propellers were a shortened version of the same device. Others were made by setting several angled blades around a central hub (boss). Modern propellers are shaped like this, and all but the biggest have two, three, or four blades. But they are still called screws.

EARLY PUSHER
This propeller is a "common screw", the most successful type of propeller up to 1860. Only then did engineers find that rounded blade tips were more efficient because they caused less vibration.

COMPOUND ENGINE
Engines like this were widely used at the end of the 19th century. They differ from simple engines in having a second cylinder that catches the steam that escapes from the first cylinder. Both cylinders then drive pistons. The next development was the triple expansion engine, with three cylinders and three pistons.

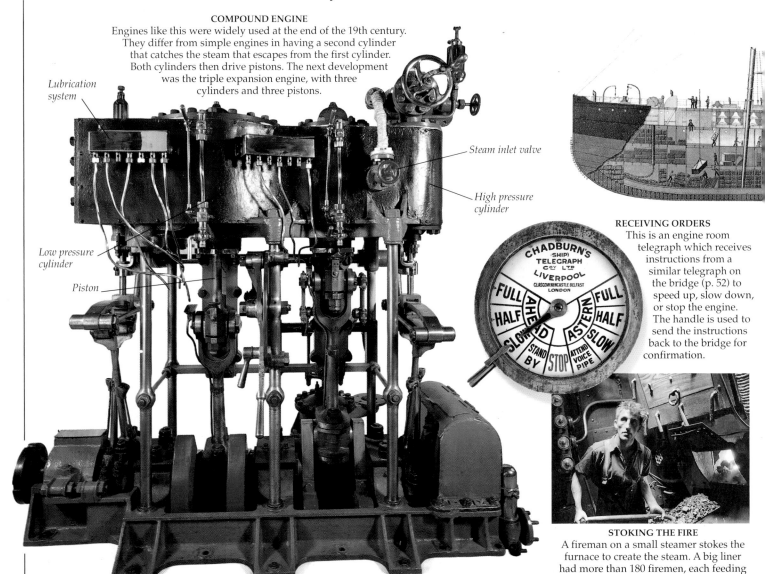

Lubrication system

Low pressure cylinder

Piston

Steam inlet valve

High pressure cylinder

RECEIVING ORDERS
This is an engine room telegraph which receives instructions from a similar telegraph on the bridge (p. 52) to speed up, slow down, or stop the engine. The handle is used to send the instructions back to the bridge for confirmation.

CHADBURN'S (SHIP) TELEGRAPH Cᴼʸ LTᴰ LIVERPOOL GLASGOW NEWCASTLE BELFAST LONDON

FULL AHEAD HALF SLOW STAND BY STOP ATTEND VOICE PIPE FULL HALF SLOW ASTERN

STOKING THE FIRE
A fireman on a small steamer stokes the furnace to create the steam. A big liner had more than 180 firemen, each feeding 5 tonnes of coal into the furnaces every day.

FIT FOR A QUEEN
Each of the *Queen Mary's* (p. 55) four propellers was 5.5 m (18 ft) in diameter and weighed 35 tonnes. Cast in London, the monster screws were then shipped to a yard on the River Clyde for fitting.

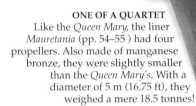

ONE OF A QUARTET
Like the *Queen Mary*, the liner *Mauretania* (pp. 54–55) had four propellers. Also made of manganese bronze, they were slightly smaller than the *Queen Mary's*. With a diameter of 5 m (16.75 ft), they weighed a mere 18.5 tonnes!

TURN OF SPEED
The *Mauretania's* propellers could turn 180 times a minute. Four bladed propellers are the most common for large ships, but two- and three-bladed ones are also made. Supertanker screws (p. 50) often have five blades.

BLADE EDGES
The blades of a propeller (in this case a common screw) are helices – like sections of a spiral.

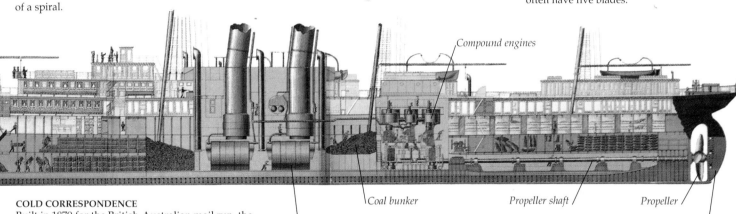

Compound engines

Coal bunker

Furnace, which heats water to form steam

Propeller shaft

Propeller

Rudder

COLD CORRESPONDENCE
Built in 1879 for the British-Australian mail run, the *Orient* was the first steamer to carry refrigerated cargo. She was a single-screw ship powered by a compound engine. On her trial she averaged over 29 km/h (18 mph).

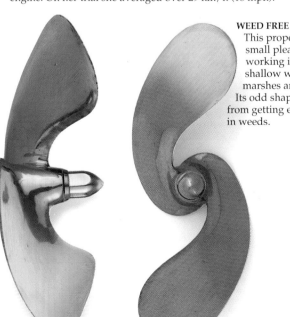

WEED FREE
This propeller is for small pleasure boats working in the shallow water of marshes and creeks. Its odd shape stops it from getting entangled in weeds.

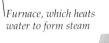

CROSSED BLADES
The two propellers on the liner *Teutonic* overlapped as they spun. But they did not interfere with each other because the port screw was positioned 1.8 m (6 ft) in front of the starboard one.

Propeller

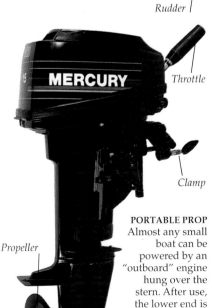

Throttle

Clamp

PORTABLE PROP
Almost any small boat can be powered by an "outboard" engine hung over the stern. After use, the lower end is pivoted up out of the water, or the whole engine can be unfastened and taken away.

39

Last days of the merchant sail

As WORLD TRADE GREW in the 19th century, there was a need for larger, faster vessels. American shipbuilders developed a new fast ship, the clipper, that plied the seven seas at record speeds. The British were soon constructing these long, sleek craft too, principally to carry tea from China. Later in the century, four-masted vessels, slower but larger, were built as well. But steamships were becoming more and more efficient, and the opening of the Suez Canal in 1869 gave them a great boost. Unable to pass through this shortcut to the Orient, sailing ships were forced to specialise in trade with other faraway places. They took coal to South America and returned to Europe with natural fertilisers, and brought wool and wheat from Australia. But by 1939 even this was uneconomic, as steamships could do the job faster and at less cost. The Age of Sail was over.

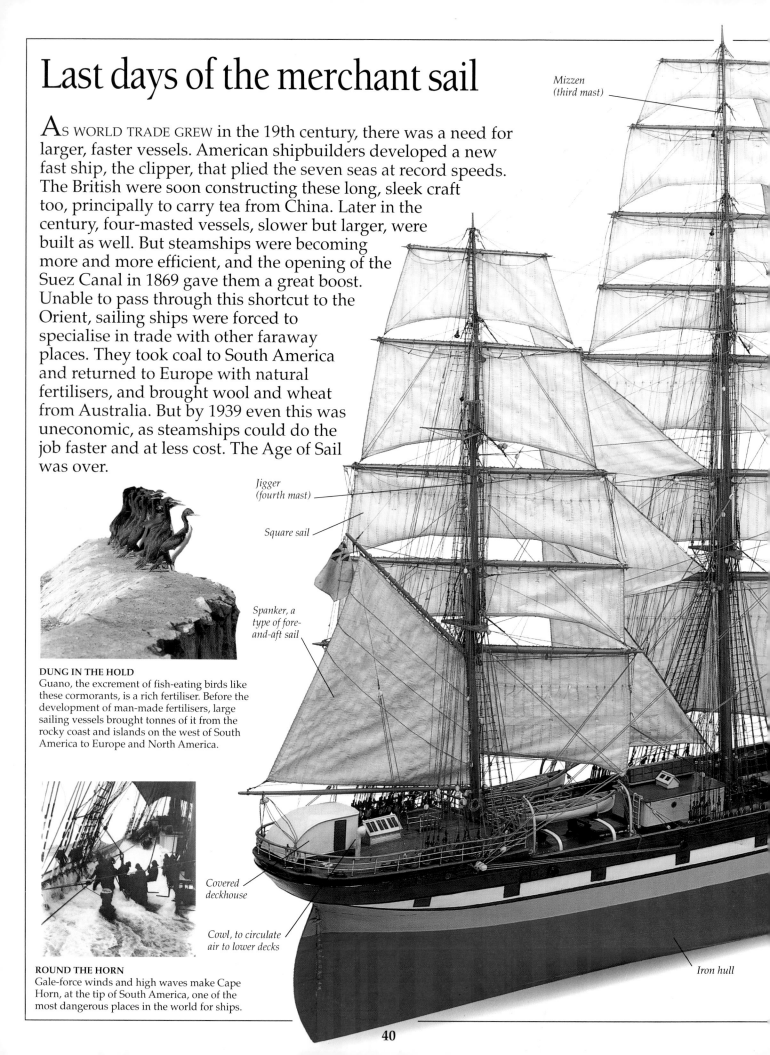

Mizzen (third mast)

Jigger (fourth mast)

Square sail

Spanker, a type of fore-and-aft sail

Covered deckhouse

Cowl, to circulate air to lower decks

Iron hull

DUNG IN THE HOLD
Guano, the excrement of fish-eating birds like these cormorants, is a rich fertiliser. Before the development of man-made fertilisers, large sailing vessels brought tonnes of it from the rocky coast and islands on the west of South America to Europe and North America.

ROUND THE HORN
Gale-force winds and high waves make Cape Horn, at the tip of South America, one of the most dangerous places in the world for ships.

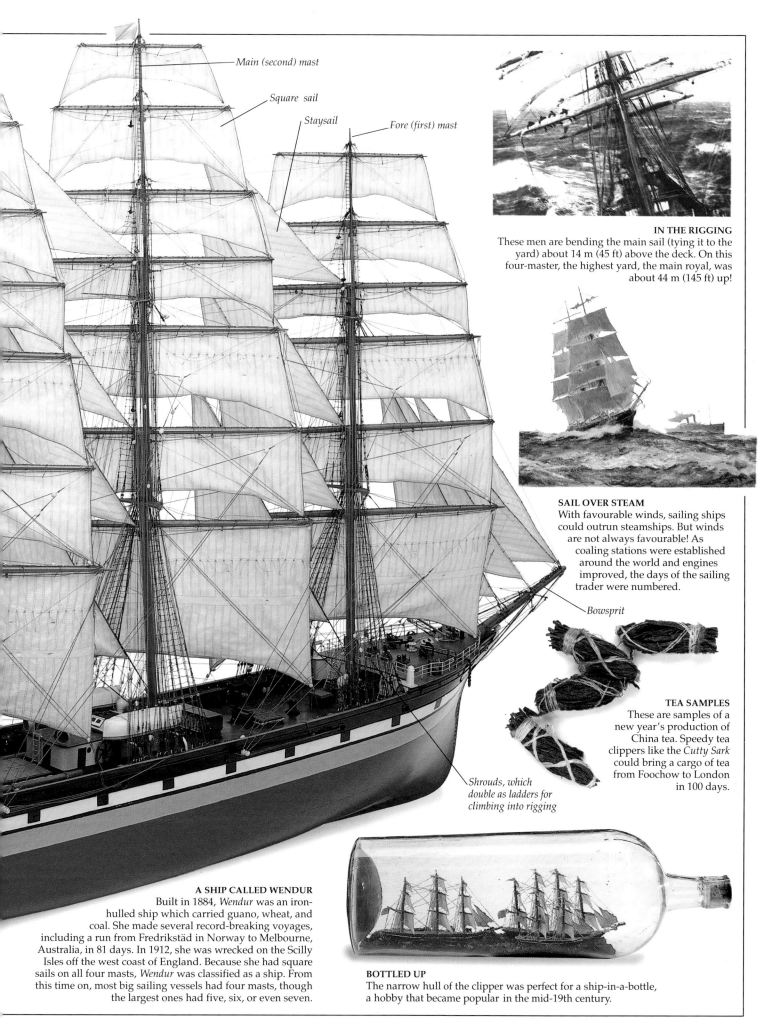

Main (second) mast

Square sail

Staysail

Fore (first) mast

IN THE RIGGING
These men are bending the main sail (tying it to the yard) about 14 m (45 ft) above the deck. On this four-master, the highest yard, the main royal, was about 44 m (145 ft) up!

SAIL OVER STEAM
With favourable winds, sailing ships could outrun steamships. But winds are not always favourable! As coaling stations were established around the world and engines improved, the days of the sailing trader were numbered.

Bowsprit

TEA SAMPLES
These are samples of a new year's production of China tea. Speedy tea clippers like the *Cutty Sark* could bring a cargo of tea from Foochow to London in 100 days.

Shrouds, which double as ladders for climbing into rigging

A SHIP CALLED WENDUR
Built in 1884, *Wendur* was an iron-hulled ship which carried guano, wheat, and coal. She made several record-breaking voyages, including a run from Fredrikstäd in Norway to Melbourne, Australia, in 81 days. In 1912, she was wrecked on the Scilly Isles off the west coast of England. Because she had square sails on all four masts, *Wendur* was classified as a ship. From this time on, most big sailing vessels had four masts, though the largest ones had five, six, or even seven.

BOTTLED UP
The narrow hull of the clipper was perfect for a ship-in-a-bottle, a hobby that became popular in the mid-19th century.

Hook, line, and sinker

Aluminium float

WHERE THERE IS WATER, THERE ARE FISH, and where there are fish, people go fishing. Fishing boats and fish-finding technology are always advancing, but the basic fishing techniques have not changed for centuries. The fish that live in the surface and middle layers of the sea often swim in large groups or shoals, and are best caught with nets. Some fishing boats take nets from the beach to the sea and back again, in a great loop which is then drawn in from the beach. Other boats – trawlers – drag nets through the water behind them. Some boats are simply used to reach deep water. Here a hook hidden in some tempting bait can reach down and snag fish that live on the seabed. Alternatively, traps can be lowered and sat on the seafloor to snare passing shellfish.

HOOKED ON FISHING
Fishing with hook and line was the most common method in the Pacific, as this drawing on a Maori paddle from New Zealand shows. Everywhere, fishing attracts the attention of hungry seabirds.

FLYING FISH
These tuna have been caught with massive hooks and strong lines. Until recently, tuna fishermen relied on nets, but protests about the many dolphins they kill accidentally have convinced many to go back to hook and line.

Spare line

Furled (rolled up) lugsail

Bait Bucket

Compass

Drainage bung

Coiled fishing line

Tub holding long line

Narrow or "tombstone" transom

Name of mother vessel

FERREIRA

GOOD COD
Cod can grow to 23 kg (50 lb). They live in deep water, but move inshore in the autumn. Cod are caught off the coasts of Norway, Iceland, and Greenland, on the Grand Banks off Newfoundland, and in the Pacific in the Bering Sea.

ROMAN BARBS
Roman subjects baited these barbed hooks and fished with them in the Bay of Naples nearly 2,000 years ago. Almost identical ones are still used today.

Four-barbed Roman fish hook

Single-barbed Roman fish hook

Grapnel, a small clawed anchor used to fix long line to the seabed

Lead weights to sink line

Mast, kept alongside sail when lowered or "shipped"

Anchor

PORTUGUESE DORY
The dory was used by American, Canadian, and European cod fishermen on the Grand Banks, off Newfoundland on the Atlantic coast of Canada. It is a cheap, flat-bottomed boat with removable thwarts, designed so that six can be stacked on the deck of a schooner (a small, fast sailing vessel) where they take up the space of one. Once the schooner arrived on the fishing grounds, the boats were launched. The two men in each boat set "long lines", long floating lines hung with many baited hooks. It was sometimes several days before a dory returned to the mother vessel to offload the catch. The Portuguese were still using this method of fishing into the 1950s, though by then their dories were equipped with radios and powered by outboard motors (p. 39).

NETTED FLOAT
Floats and weights are used to keep nets hanging in the water. The netting around this glass float protects it while the net is pulled in and out. Before plastics became widespread in the 1960s, floats were usually made of glass or cork.

Anchor rope

Cork float for marking where the long line has been set

Removable thwart

Rowing crutch

Bailer

Oar

SAILING TRAWLER
To tow a heavy net through the water, sailing trawlers had to be solidly built with a large sail area. Fishing under sail was still a widespread activity as late as 1926, when this boat, *Vigilance*, was built. On her sail, she carries the registration number of her home port, Brixham, on England's south coast.

NETTING THE CATCH
Nets bursting with sardines are being dragged on board these French fishing boats. Small fish like sardines and pilchards are caught with fine mesh nets, which fishermen use to encircle them.

CRABMEN
These 19th-century fishermen are mending their crab pots, which had only just been developed. The pots are made of hazel loops and bars set into an oak frame which carries an iron weight. They are baited, roped together, and sunk to the seabed, to be retrieved with their catch the next day.

LOBSTER TRAP
This willow pot, like the crab pot, will be baited and weighted and dropped to sit on the seabed. The lobster will enter through the opening – the "eye"– but will not be able to escape. Some lobster boats carry up to 700 of these pots.

Continued on next page

Tangling and scooping

Nets come in a multitude of materials and sizes. The people of New Guinea once fished with hand-held scoops made of strong spiders' webs, while modern commercial trawlers drag synthetic-fibre nets many kilometres long. But all nets work in one of two ways. Some have fairly big holes, so that fish trying to swim through them become entangled in the net. The most common of these are called gill nets, because they catch fish by the gills. Other nets are finer, and simply scoop up whole shoals of fish. Some, like the whitebait net, are fixed in place and rely on the fish swimming into them. Others, like seine (encircling) and trawling nets, are dragged through the sea after the shoals.

IN THE BAG
Full of fish, this is the "cod end" of a trawling net. It is a detachable bag to which long wings of netting are attached. Dragged through the water by ropes tied to these wings, the net is like a giant funnel.

A STERN VIEW
This German trawler, *Österreich*, has one large net which is hauled out of the water by winches mounted on the stern. Such "stern trawling" is a very common and productive fishing method in Northern Europe. Catches of 80 tonnes of herring in 20 minutes are not unusual.

STOWBOATERS
These river fishermen are catching small fish called whitebait with a stow net. Like a trawl net, it is funnel shaped. But instead of being dragged through the water, it is anchored to the riverbed, to trap fish as they swim by.

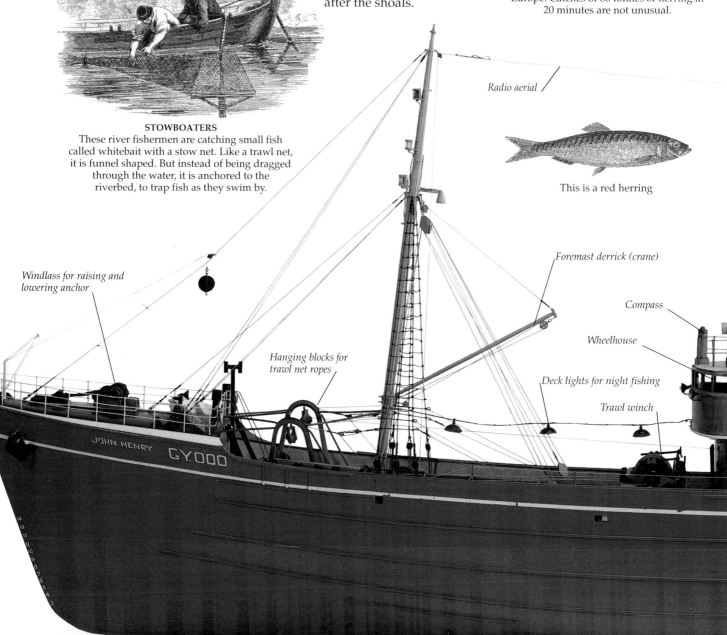

Radio aerial

This is a red herring

Foremast derrick (crane)

Compass

Wheelhouse

Deck lights for night fishing

Trawl winch

Hanging blocks for trawl net ropes

Windlass for raising and lowering anchor

JOHN HENRY GY.000

DOUBLE TAKE
Shrimps are often caught by a method called twin-rig trawling. This French trawler shows how it is done, by pulling a trawl net from each of her two outriggers. One net will be towed about 50 m (150 ft) behind the other. A third, very small trawl net – the try net – may also be towed from the stern.

GUTTING
This man is "gutting" or "cleaning" a tuna – removing its internal organs. If a boat is out for a long time or has limited refrigeration, the catch will be gutted at sea.

MAINTAINING THE GEAR
Fishermen in waterproof "sou'westers" repair their nets. Nets must be light, so they are easy to handle and so that fish do not see them. But light nets are also fragile and need to be constantly mended. Gill nets in particular are frequently ripped by fish too large to be caught by the gills. Bottom trawls, nets which are dragged along the seabed, are often torn by rocks and wrecks.

SHOOTING FROM THE SIDE
The *John Henry* is a side trawler. She does not have a working area on her stern, as *Österreich* does. Instead, the net is shot (thrown out) and hauled in on the open deck in front of the wheelhouse. Trawlers like her from Grimsby in England netted cod off Iceland and Greenland in the 1940s and '50s. They had oil-fired steam engines. Within a few years, more efficient diesel-powered fishing boats appeared, but many skippers prefer steam because it gives a limitless supply of hot water for de-icing the boat and her gear in freezing winter weather.

TAKING THE BAIT
These Peruvian fishermen are hauling in a net bursting with anchovetas. They will then use these small anchovies as bait for catching tuna.

Mizzen light

Radar scanner

Funnel

Hanging blocks

Lifeboat "davit" or holder

GY.000

Rudder

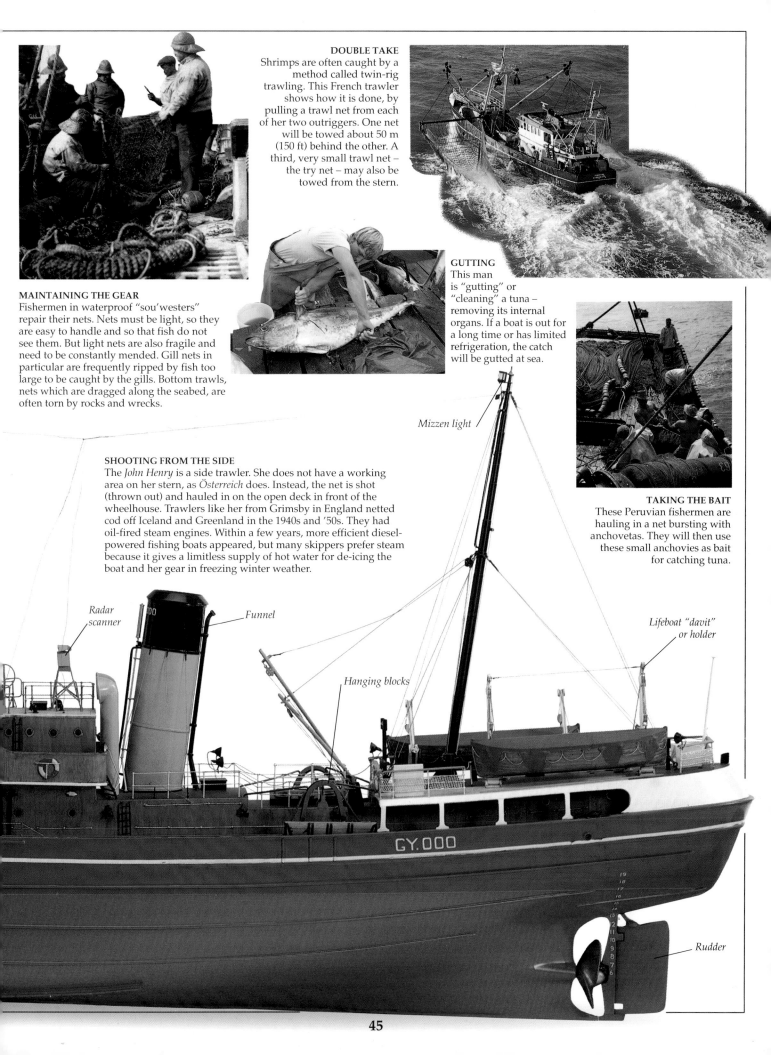

Building in iron and steel

BREAK OUT
THE BUBBLY
When a ship is
launched, she is
christened with a
bottle of champagne
smashed over
her bow.

Hundreds of workers, from rivetters, plumbers, and electricians to painters, engineers, blacksmiths, and carpenters, are employed in a shipyard. The first iron ships were constructed in much the same way as skeleton-built wooden ships (pp. 18–19). The internal structure of the ship was erected first and then the shell was fastened around it. The metal plates were even rivetted together in much the same way as the planks of a wooden boat (p. 19). And iron and steel ships were still built in the open air, as wooden ships had been for centuries. But since 1945, welding has replaced riveting. Computers are now widely used to automate plate-cutting and welding, and many ships are built in sections which are then fastened together. When the ship is finally launched, it hits the water as an empty metal shell. Then the work of "fitting out", preparing the vessel for a lifetime at sea, begins.

ON THE STOCKS
To allow easy access and an easy launch, the hull of a ship under construction is held in place by wooden supports called stocks. This picture shows the luxurious liner the *Aquitania* (pp. 54–57) in 1913. She was launched, stern first, into the River Clyde in Scotland a few weeks later.

Cranes used to hoist masts

Vessel being fitted out

Timber pond, where wood for masts is kept moist

Riveting shed

SHIP FACTORY
This is the Denny Brothers' shipbuilding yard at Dumbarton in Scotland in 1900. The Dennys were pioneers of steel ship construction who tested proposed ships with models in an experimental tank.

Spar shop

Plumbers' shop

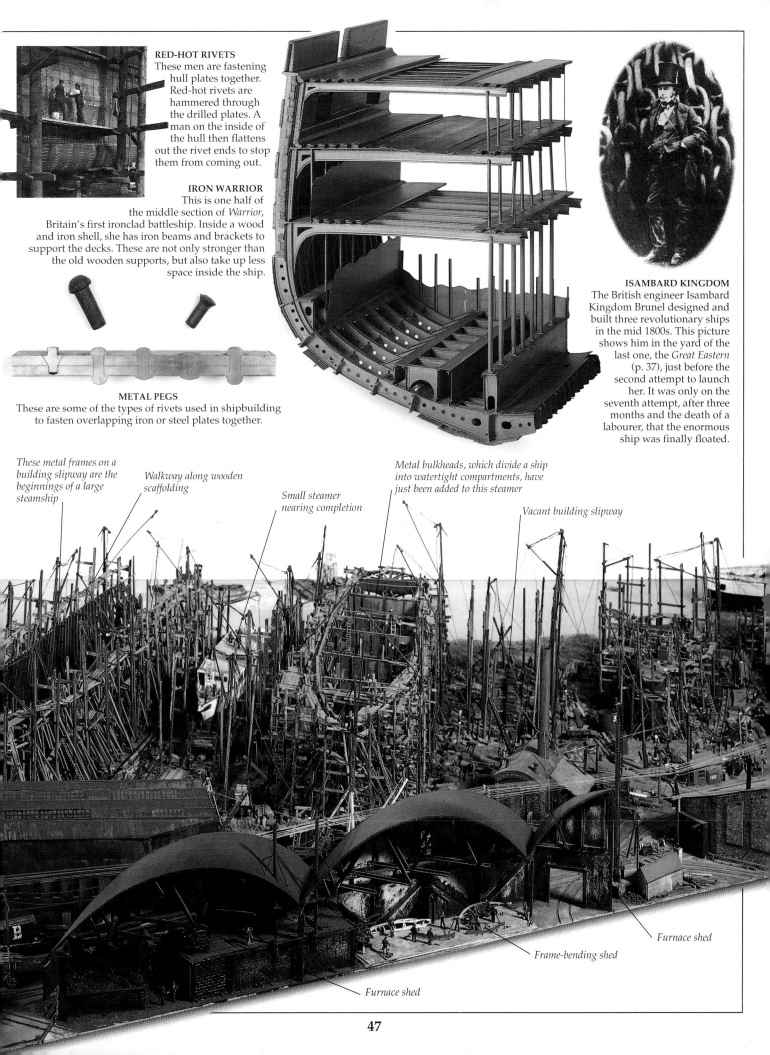

RED-HOT RIVETS
These men are fastening hull plates together. Red-hot rivets are hammered through the drilled plates. A man on the inside of the hull then flattens out the rivet ends to stop them from coming out.

IRON WARRIOR
This is one half of the middle section of *Warrior*, Britain's first ironclad battleship. Inside a wood and iron shell, she has iron beams and brackets to support the decks. These are not only stronger than the old wooden supports, but also take up less space inside the ship.

METAL PEGS
These are some of the types of rivets used in shipbuilding to fasten overlapping iron or steel plates together.

ISAMBARD KINGDOM
The British engineer Isambard Kingdom Brunel designed and built three revolutionary ships in the mid 1800s. This picture shows him in the yard of the last one, the *Great Eastern* (p. 37), just before the second attempt to launch her. It was only on the seventh attempt, after three months and the death of a labourer, that the enormous ship was finally floated.

These metal frames on a building slipway are the beginnings of a large steamship

Walkway along wooden scaffolding

Small steamer nearing completion

Metal bulkheads, which divide a ship into watertight compartments, have just been added to this steamer

Vacant building slipway

Furnace shed

Frame-bending shed

Furnace shed

Tramping the seas

T HOUGH AEROPLANES have taken passenger traffic away from ships, they have had little impact on the carrying of cargo. More than 95 per cent of goods are still transported by sea. Until recently, most cargo ships carried a wide range of goods. Early steamships were called "tramps" because they chugged from port to port carrying all sorts of cargo with no fixed route. There are still a few tramps today, but there are also many very specialised vessels, built to carry just one type of cargo or perform one particular job. With rising fuel, crew, and cargo-handling costs, there is a continual drive to develop more efficient and economical ships.

FLAGGING OUT
Because of heavy taxes in Europe and North America, 12 per cent of the world's merchant ships are registered under the Panamian flag.

BACK TO SAILS
Launched in 1980, the Japanese *Shin Aitoku Maru* was the world's first motor tanker to be fitted with computer-controlled sails. Her fuel bill is about ten per cent less than a tanker of the same size with no sails.

COLD CARRIER
The Norwegian *Norman Lady* is built to carry 87,600 m³ (3,092,300 ft³) of liquified natural gas in special spherical tanks. Because the gas occupies a lot less space in liquid form, it is chilled to a temperature of -163°C (-261°F). The nickel steel tanks are strong enough to withstand the enormous pressure and are completely insulated from the rest of the ship so the extreme cold does not cause the steel to fracture.

TRAMPING INTO THE RED SEA
With a searchlight mounted at the bow, the *Springwell* is ready to pass through the Suez Canal. At sea, the light would be shipped and her cargo hatches would be covered with canvas tarpaulins. This tramp carried coal from Britain to bunker stations – places where ships could take on coal – all around the world until she was sunk by a torpedo in 1916. Miraculously, all her crew survived.

Poop deck, the third "island" on a three-island steamer

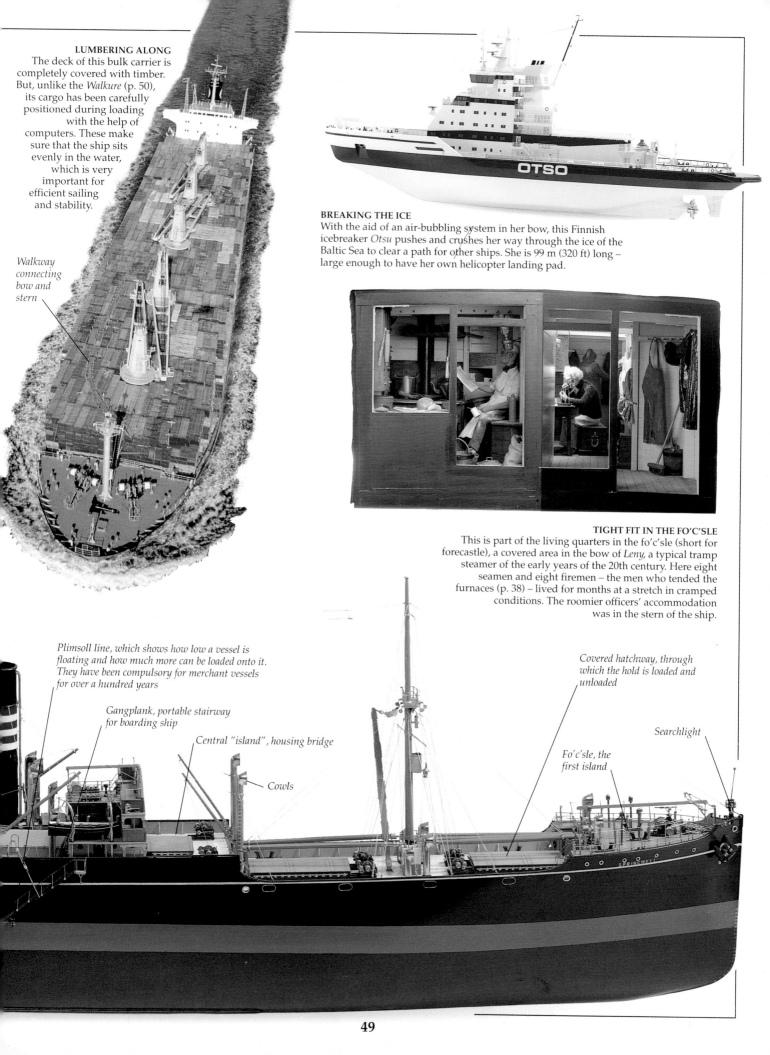

LUMBERING ALONG
The deck of this bulk carrier is completely covered with timber. But, unlike the *Walkure* (p. 50), its cargo has been carefully positioned during loading with the help of computers. These make sure that the ship sits evenly in the water, which is very important for efficient sailing and stability.

Walkway connecting bow and stern

BREAKING THE ICE
With the aid of an air-bubbling system in her bow, this Finnish icebreaker *Otsu* pushes and crushes her way through the ice of the Baltic Sea to clear a path for other ships. She is 99 m (320 ft) long – large enough to have her own helicopter landing pad.

TIGHT FIT IN THE FO'C'SLE
This is part of the living quarters in the fo'c'sle (short for forecastle), a covered area in the bow of *Leny,* a typical tramp steamer of the early years of the 20th century. Here eight seamen and eight firemen – the men who tended the furnaces (p. 38) – lived for months at a stretch in cramped conditions. The roomier officers' accommodation was in the stern of the ship.

Plimsoll line, which shows how low a vessel is floating and how much more can be loaded onto it. They have been compulsory for merchant vessels for over a hundred years

Gangplank, portable stairway for boarding ship

Central "island", housing bridge

Cowls

Covered hatchway, through which the hold is loaded and unloaded

Searchlight

Fo'c'sle, the first island

49

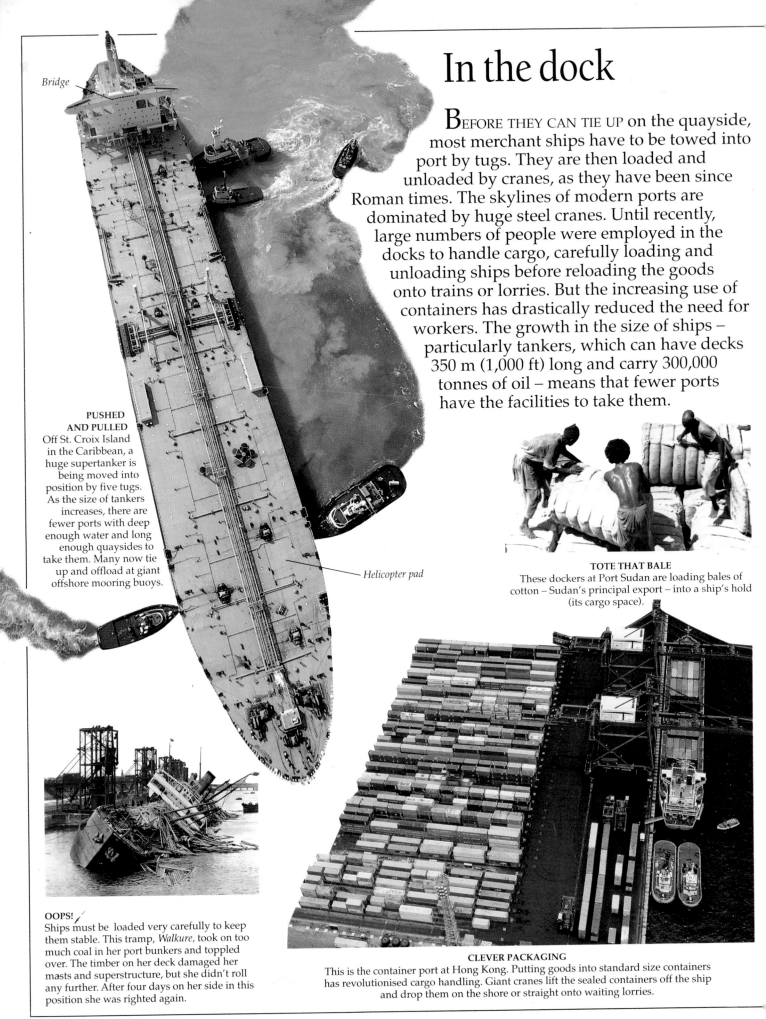

In the dock

BEFORE THEY CAN TIE UP on the quayside, most merchant ships have to be towed into port by tugs. They are then loaded and unloaded by cranes, as they have been since Roman times. The skylines of modern ports are dominated by huge steel cranes. Until recently, large numbers of people were employed in the docks to handle cargo, carefully loading and unloading ships before reloading the goods onto trains or lorries. But the increasing use of containers has drastically reduced the need for workers. The growth in the size of ships – particularly tankers, which can have decks 350 m (1,000 ft) long and carry 300,000 tonnes of oil – means that fewer ports have the facilities to take them.

Bridge

PUSHED AND PULLED
Off St. Croix Island in the Caribbean, a huge supertanker is being moved into position by five tugs. As the size of tankers increases, there are fewer ports with deep enough water and long enough quaysides to take them. Many now tie up and offload at giant offshore mooring buoys.

Helicopter pad

TOTE THAT BALE
These dockers at Port Sudan are loading bales of cotton – Sudan's principal export – into a ship's hold (its cargo space).

OOPS!
Ships must be loaded very carefully to keep them stable. This tramp, *Walkure*, took on too much coal in her port bunkers and toppled over. The timber on her deck damaged her masts and superstructure, but she didn't roll any further. After four days on her side in this position she was righted again.

CLEVER PACKAGING
This is the container port at Hong Kong. Putting goods into standard size containers has revolutionised cargo handling. Giant cranes lift the sealed containers off the ship and drop them on the shore or straight onto waiting lorries.

DOCKERS' TOOLS

Hooks like these are used to grab hold of packages swung to and from a ship by cranes.

FROM STEAMSHIP TO STEAM TRAIN
Most ports are well served by train links. In this poster advertising the South Wales Docks near Cardiff, a steamship's cargo of timber is being loaded into the freight cars of a waiting steam train.

FENDING OFF
This rope fender is hung from the side of a boat to stop it from scraping against the quay or against other boats. Old tyres do the same job.

AND ON THE INSIDE...
Even inside a container, goods must be packed in manageable units, like this Japanese tea chest.

ROPED TO THE QUAY
Ships (and ropes) may have got a lot bigger, but the basic method of tying them to bollards on the quay has not changed for centuries.

Wheelhouse

Towing rope

DANUBE VI

Propeller in well

Rudder

MOVER OF THE MIGHTY
In restricted waterways like ports, large ships cannot manoeuvre easily and must rely on tugs to tow them. This one, *Danube VI*, worked on the River Thames in the 1930s. Modern towing tugs are very similar, with a large hook behind the wheelhouse and a clear deck at the stern. Liners like the *Mauretania* (pp. 54–55) had to be moved by six tugs.

DOWN IN THE HOLD
The cargo hold of this freighter is packed with small loose bundles of cocoa which must be loaded and unloaded by dockers.

ANCHORS AWAY
A ship at rest is buffetted by winds, tides, and currents. Whether stopping for the night or waiting for a berth in port, the captain drops an anchor to fix the vessel to the seabed. The first anchors were stones or baskets full of rocks. Modern anchors come in many shapes and sizes.

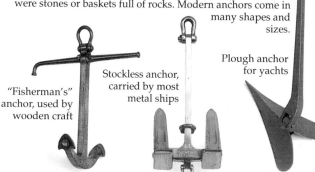

"Fisherman's" anchor, used by wooden craft

Stockless anchor, carried by most metal ships

Plough anchor for yachts

On the bridge

THE BRIDGE OR WHEELHOUSE of this fire-fighting boat houses the vessel's navigational and steering instruments, as well as the controls for its engines and water pumps, all in one small area. Like all bridges, it is positioned for good visibility. Old sailing ships were controlled from a raised deck on the stern, the quarterdeck. But the bridge on a steam or motor ship is farther forwards, so that the people at the controls are well clear of the smoke from the funnels and can see where they are going.

PORT LIGHT
A red light is always hung on the port side (left as you face the bow) of a ship, while a green light is hung on the starboard (right). In fog or darkness, these tell other ships which way a vessel is going.

DEAD SLOW AHEAD
With a wire and chain mechanism, this "telegraph" from a large steamship was used to transmit orders from the bridge to the engine room, where there was a similar dial (p. 38). The fire boat does not need a telegraph because the men in the wheelhouse have direct control of the engines.

Switches used for sending fire-fighting orders to engine room

Pump gauges

Wheel to turn rudder and steer boat

Compass gimbal, metal ball which counteracts magnetism of steel boat

Imperial Russian eagle

Lamp

Compass and card sit in here

COMPASS HOLDER
This is the housing or "binnacle" for the compass card shown on the left. The brass top is pivoted so that it will roll as the ship rolls, thus keeping the compass flat. At the very top is a lamp to illuminate the compass at night.

WAYFINDER
This is a compass card from a 19th-century ship of the Russian Imperial Navy. On most land compasses, the needle moves around the card. But on a maritime compass, the needle is fixed to the underside of the card so that both move.

Green starboard light, to indicate right side of boat

When the Turk's head knot is in this position, the rudder is in line with the hull and the boat is going straight ahead

Panel with engine gauges

Port and starboard engine throttles and gears, to allow boat to manoeuvre in tight spots

Radar with shield to keep out daylight

Compass

Rudder angle indicator

Luxurious liners

As STEAMSHIPS DEVELOPED, they could travel to other continents faster than any vessel under sail. Special ships were built to carry large numbers of passengers across the Atlantic and Pacific. These ships were called liners, because they worked regular routes or lines. The Golden Age of the liner was in the 1920s and 1930s, when enormous, luxurious ships sailed the world. For the richest passengers who travelled First Class, these ships rivalled the best hotels on land. There was great competition among the shipping companies to provide the quickest service across the Atlantic. The fastest ship was said to hold the "Blue Riband". The most successful company was the Cunard Line, which built a number of record-breaking ships. But by the 1950s, liners could not compete with jet airliners for speed or price. One by one, most of these great ships have been retired and broken up for scrap.

COFFEE SHOP
This is the elegant verandah café on Canadian Pacific's *Empress of Australia* in the 1930s.

WATER ON WATER
In 1911, *Olympic*, sister ship to the *Titanic* (p. 59), became the first liner to have a swimming pool. Many liners had both indoor and outdoor pools

GERMAN CHAMPION
The *Bremen* was one of many fast German liners which rivalled Cunard's ships for the Blue Riband. She succeeded in capturing it from the *Mauretania* on her maiden (first) voyage in 1929.

One of four funnels, each expelling the exhaust fumes of one of four boiler rooms

Radio aerial

First Class promenade decks

Observation room

Bridge

Cowl

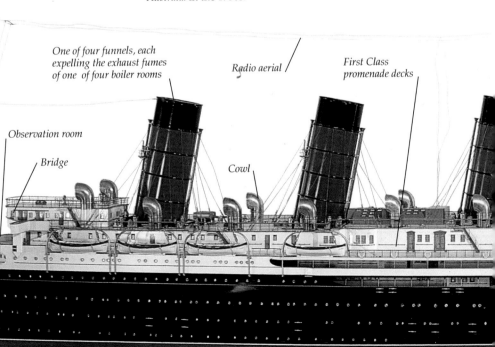

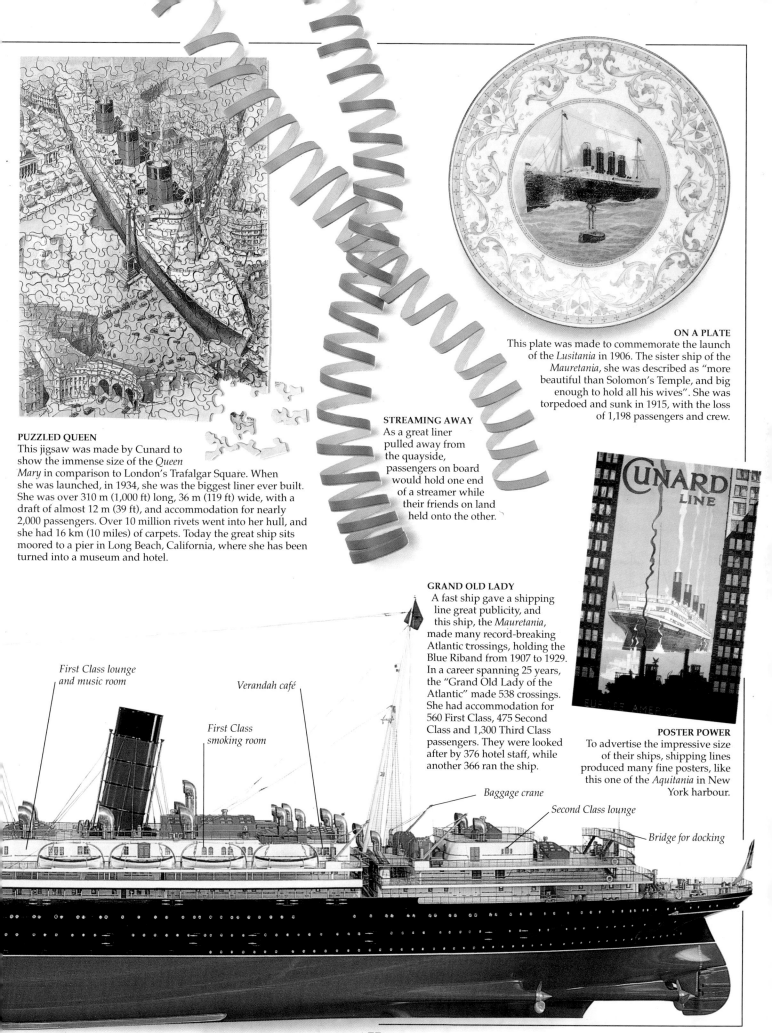

PUZZLED QUEEN

This jigsaw was made by Cunard to show the immense size of the *Queen Mary* in comparison to London's Trafalgar Square. When she was launched, in 1934, she was the biggest liner ever built. She was over 310 m (1,000 ft) long, 36 m (119 ft) wide, with a draft of almost 12 m (39 ft), and accommodation for nearly 2,000 passengers. Over 10 million rivets went into her hull, and she had 16 km (10 miles) of carpets. Today the great ship sits moored to a pier in Long Beach, California, where she has been turned into a museum and hotel.

ON A PLATE

This plate was made to commemorate the launch of the *Lusitania* in 1906. The sister ship of the *Mauretania*, she was described as "more beautiful than Solomon's Temple, and big enough to hold all his wives". She was torpedoed and sunk in 1915, with the loss of 1,198 passengers and crew.

STREAMING AWAY

As a great liner pulled away from the quayside, passengers on board would hold one end of a streamer while their friends on land held onto the other.

GRAND OLD LADY

A fast ship gave a shipping line great publicity, and this ship, the *Mauretania*, made many record-breaking Atlantic crossings, holding the Blue Riband from 1907 to 1929. In a career spanning 25 years, the "Grand Old Lady of the Atlantic" made 538 crossings. She had accommodation for 560 First Class, 475 Second Class and 1,300 Third Class passengers. They were looked after by 376 hotel staff, while another 366 ran the ship.

POSTER POWER

To advertise the impressive size of their ships, shipping lines produced many fine posters, like this one of the *Aquitania* in New York harbour.

First Class lounge and music room

Verandah café

First Class smoking room

Baggage crane

Second Class lounge

Bridge for docking

Continued on next page

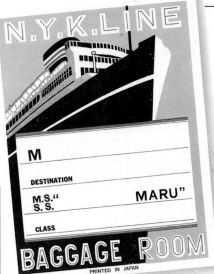

LINER LUGGAGE

This is a baggage ticket of the Nippon Yusen Kaisha Line, or "the Japanese Mail Steamship Company", which ran from 1885 to 1960. It took many Japanese immigrants to Hawaii.

SAFETY AT SEA

Like all modern liners, the Italian Line's *Michelangelo* has lifeboats for all her passengers and crew, a total of nearly 2,000 people. Rigorous safety standards were introduced after the *Titanic* disaster (p. 59), and all passengers must do lifeboat drills.

JAPANESE GIANT

Founded in the 1880s, the OSK line is now part of Mitsui-OSK, second only to P&O as the largest shipping line in the world.

GENTLEMEN PREFER BLONDES

In a scene from this popular 1953 film, the American actress Marilyn Monroe looks through a porthole. These round windows weaken the steel structure of a liner much less than rectangular ones.

LUNCH ON A LINER

This menu was printed for the liner company Peninsular and Orient (P&O), which specialised in travel to the Far East.

CABIN COMFORTS

Maple panelling and a pair of portholes are among the features of a First Class double cabin on board the *Empress of Canada*. Launched in 1960, this Canadian Pacific liner could carry 200 First Class and 856 Tourist Class passengers.

Hot water jug

LUXURY CRUISER

Sailing in style continues today on luxury cruise ships like the *Crown Princess*, launched in 1989. These ships are built for holiday makers, not travellers.

Coffee pot

Tea pot

TEA AND COFFEE

This coffee and tea service was used on Orient Line ships sailing to and from Australia in the 1960s.

DUTCH PRIDE
Built in 1929, the *Statendam* was the flagship of the Holland-America Line. This company's reputation for cleanliness earned it the nickname "the Spotless Fleet".

FIRST SIGHT
Since it was erected in 1886, the Statue of Liberty has greeted passengers arriving by boat in New York harbour.

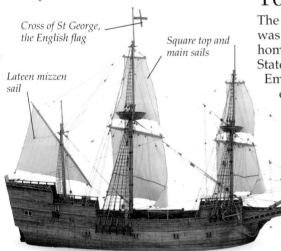

Cross of St George, the English flag

Square top and main sails

Lateen mizzen sail

EARLY ARRIVALS
This tiny ship, only about 40 m (125 ft) long, arrived in America on 11 November 1620, having left England 67 days before. It was the *Mayflower* and on board were 102 Puritans, members of a religious sect who had fled persecution at home. They founded the first permanent European colony in what is now the USA.

To a new life

The cheapest accommodation of the great liners was largely occupied by emigrants, leaving their homelands to make a new life in the United States, Canada, Australia, and New Zealand. Emigration to North America had begun much earlier, in the 17th century. Many of the first settlers left Europe because of religious or political persecution. So did later emigrants, like those from Russia and Eastern Europe. Others, from Ireland and Italy in particular, left to escape famine and poverty. Still others came to the "New World" – the Americas – because it offered more opportunities than the old. Emigration continues today, on a smaller scale but for much the same reasons.

OLD AND NEW
On this poster, the *Mauretania* steams past a sailing ship. While it might take weeks to sail across the Atlantic, the liner could make the crossing in 5 days.

TRAMPING ACROSS THE OCEAN
In the short film *The Immigrant*, the actor Charlie Chaplin plays a tramp on board a steamship bound for America. Chaplin himself had left the poverty of a London slum and made his career and fortune in the United States.

BOAT PEOPLE
Political events sometimes force people to take great risks in leaving their home countries. These Vietnamese refugees have paid large sums of money for a dangerous passage on a small boat. With luck, they will reach Hong Kong.

LEAVING HOME
On the quay at Genoa in 1901, Italians who have fled war in the north wait with their few possessions to board steamers bound for America.

TURNED AWAY
After 1945, many Jews left Europe for Palestine. The people on one crowded ship were turned away by the British authorities and had to return to Germany. The incident caused an international outcry, and was featured in a 1961 film. Like the ship, the film was called *Exodus*, which means leaving.

S.O.S. (Save Our Souls!)

THREE DOTS, THREE DASHES, AND THREE DOTS is the Morse Code signal for S.O.S. – short for Save Our Souls, a desperate plea for help from other ships or the shore. Every maritime nation has a rescue service and maintains lighthouses and lightships to warn sailors of dangerous rocks and shallows. Professional sailors take all precautions they can. Ships are equipped with radios, radar, depth-sounders, and emergency flares, and since the *Titanic* disaster they are obliged to carry lifeboats and lifejackets for all on board. But the sea has not been conquered, and its bed is still littered with wrecks. Ships go down every year; some even vanish without trace. And because ships are now larger than ever before and carry more dangerous cargo, disasters can be much greater.

CASTAWAY
Robinson Crusoe was based on the true story of Alexander Selkirk, who was abandoned on a Pacific island in 1704.

TO THE RESCUE
The popular beaches of Australia are patrolled by lifesavers who are always ready to rescue swimmers or surfers who get into difficulties. Their rowing boats are specially designed to ride over the high surf.

SEA DEVIL
Mermaids were bad omens. A sailor who saw one was sure his ship would soon be wrecked. He may have really been looking at a sea mammal called a dugong.

BELLOWING OUT
Fog is a great danger at sea, for it obscures rocks, lighthouses, and other ships from view. The handle on this portable fog horn pumps a set of bellows to produce a wailing sound, which alerts other vessels to the ship's presence.

Hand-held flares

Foghorn

FLARES AND WAILS
This fog horn uses a a cylinder of compressed air to make an ear-piercing noise. As well as warning of a ship's presence, it can be used to signal simple messages. Flares are distress signals and help to guide searching rescue craft.

ABANDONED SHIP
In November 1872, a month after she left New York, the *Mary Celeste* was found drifting in the Atlantic with no-one on board. Her tender was missing and she looked as if she had been abandoned in a great hurry. There are many theories as to what happened. There may have been a mutiny, with the crew turning against their captain. Or the crew may have fled because they feared her cargo of alcohol was about to explode. Either way, no-one knows what happened to the ten people on board, who included a two-year-old girl.

RESCUE THE RESCUERS
Lifeboat men risk their lives to save other sailors, but because they are called out when the sea is most dangerous, disaster can strike them too.

LIGHT SHIP
Light ships are anchored in treacherous spots where a lighthouse cannot be built. This one is moored in the North Sea 32 km (20 miles) off the English coast. A crew of seven lives on board. Her light is 12 m (40 ft) above sea level and can be seen from 38 km (24 miles) away. It is a "dumb" ship, meaning that it has no engine and had to be towed to the Kentish Knock, a dangerous sandbank.

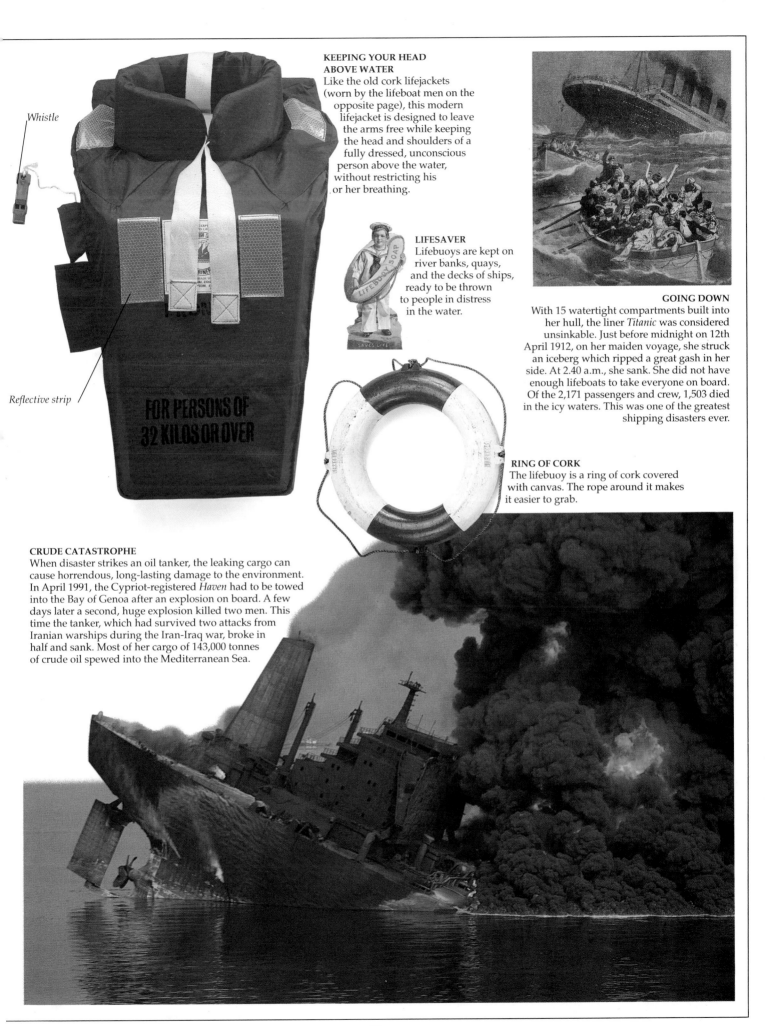

Whistle

Reflective strip

FOR PERSONS OF
32 KILOS OR OVER

**KEEPING YOUR HEAD
ABOVE WATER**
Like the old cork lifejackets
(worn by the lifeboat men on the
opposite page), this modern
lifejacket is designed to leave
the arms free while keeping
the head and shoulders of a
fully dressed, unconscious
person above the water,
without restricting his
or her breathing.

LIFESAVER
Lifebuoys are kept on
river banks, quays,
and the decks of ships,
ready to be thrown
to people in distress
in the water.

LIFEBUOY SOAP

SAVES LIFE

GOING DOWN
With 15 watertight compartments built into
her hull, the liner *Titanic* was considered
unsinkable. Just before midnight on 12th
April 1912, on her maiden voyage, she struck
an iceberg which ripped a great gash in her
side. At 2.40 a.m., she sank. She did not have
enough lifeboats to take everyone on board.
Of the 2,171 passengers and crew, 1,503 died
in the icy waters. This was one of the greatest
shipping disasters ever.

RING OF CORK
The lifebuoy is a ring of cork covered
with canvas. The rope around it makes
it easier to grab.

CRUDE CATASTROPHE
When disaster strikes an oil tanker, the leaking cargo can
cause horrendous, long-lasting damage to the environment.
In April 1991, the Cypriot-registered *Haven* had to be towed
into the Bay of Genoa after an explosion on board. A few
days later a second, huge explosion killed two men. This
time the tanker, which had survived two attacks from
Iranian warships during the Iran-Iraq war, broke in
half and sank. Most of her cargo of 143,000 tonnes
of crude oil spewed into the Mediterranean Sea.

Yachts for cruising

WINGED VICTOR
In 1983, this secret, revolutionary keel helped *Australia II* to become the first yacht to capture the America's Cup from the Americans.

VIEW FROM THE TOP
This is the Swiss 25-m (81-ft) yacht *Merit*, which finished third in the 1989–1990 Whitbread Round the World Race. Her crew of 15 completed the gruelling circumnavigation in just over 69 days at sea.

In 1851, the New York Yacht Club's *America* (p. 7) beat the 15 best yachts in Britain in a race around the Isle of Wight, off the south coast of England. The victorious club issued a challenge to the rest of the world's sailors, offering the cup they had won to any yacht that could beat *America*. So began the most famous yacht race of all, the America's Cup. Yacht races were being held two centuries before this. The first yacht club was founded in 1720, at Cork in Ireland. At first yachting was the sport of the very wealthy. Even today, the yachts that fight for the America's Cup and the Whitbread Round the World Race cost millions of dollars. A major industry devotes millions more to the search for faster, more efficient sailboats, testing new materials and designs. This is profitable because yacht racing is now enjoyed by a lot more people. There are many relatively cheap, mass-produced yachts on the market. Some of these race against each other. Others just take their owners to sea, for the pure pleasure of sailing.

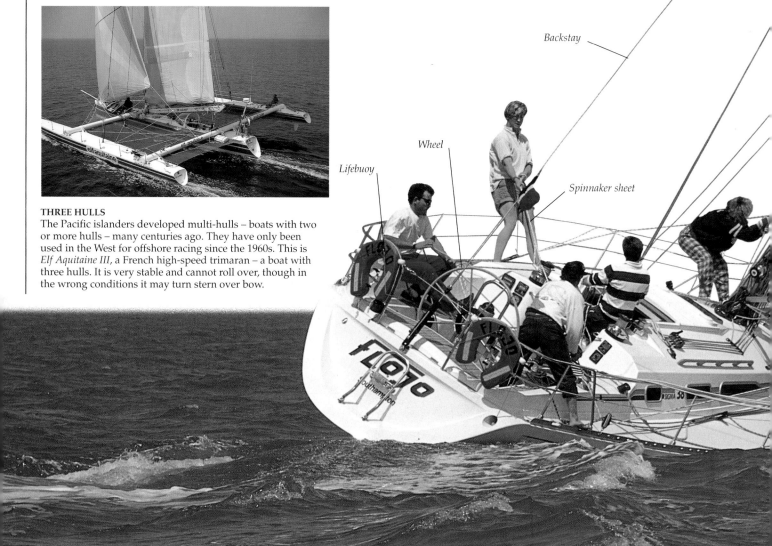

THREE HULLS
The Pacific islanders developed multi-hulls – boats with two or more hulls – many centuries ago. They have only been used in the West for offshore racing since the 1960s. This is *Elf Aquitaine III*, a French high-speed trimaran – a boat with three hulls. It is very stable and cannot roll over, though in the wrong conditions it may turn stern over bow.

Backstay

Wheel

Lifebuoy

Spinnaker sheet

Registration number – the letter "K" indicates that the boat is registered in Britain

Mast made of lightweight alloy

Shroud

Spreader

Wooden batten to stiffen sail

Mainsail, made (like jib) of a synthetic material called dacron

Genoa, a large kind of jib

K-23

K-8308

Spinnaker, made of lightweight nylon

IN NEED OF A TRIM
The spinnaker (p. 23) is making this Sigma 38 yacht heel to starboard. This can be cured by altering course slightly, or by moving the weight of the crew to the windward side. Both the jib, which has become entangled, and the mainsail, which is flapping, need trimming (adjusting). None of these difficulties are too serious, however. Yachts like this are very seaworthy and rarely capsize. They bring the excitement of yacht racing (and gentle cruising) to many more people than can afford an international racing yacht.

Learning the ropes

YOU CAN LEARN TO SAIL in a weekend. If you do, you may well spend the rest of your life perfecting your technique. There are now countless sailing clubs around the world, by the sea, on lakes, and on reservoirs. Sailing is becoming more and more popular both as a serious sport and as a pastime, offering not only challenge and excitement but also good exercise in the fresh air. To be a good competitive sailor, you must be very fit. It is not a dangerous sport provided simple rules on safety and clothing are followed. Like any other sport, the best way to begin is to learn the basic points and skills on a course. There are many organisations which run sailing schools, and hundreds of different types of small boats. Many people start to sail in simple boats like the one-person Optimist and then gradually move on to bigger and faster boats. Boats without decks used for pleasure sailing are usually called dinghies (from an Indian word for boat). The first dinghies were made of wood, but today most are built of moulded plastic, which means they are hard-wearing and do not need much maintenance. Dinghies can be expensive to buy, but many clubs hire them out.

DRESSED TO GET WET
Even on the warmest day, it is possible to get very cold and wet when sailing. It is very important to dress properly for the sport.

Light, waterproof nylon suit can be worn over warm clothes on a cold day

Spritsail, made of dacron

Boom

Elasticised wrists and neck keep water out

KEEPING AFLOAT
Most sailing clubs insist that buoyancy aids like this vest are worn at all times. They are warm and comfortable, but do not give as much support as a lifejacket (p. 59).

Transom stern

Tiller

SUITABLE
A good dinghy suit keeps out both the wind and the water. Bright colours like these are not only fashionable but also have a practical purpose. Should a dinghy capsize, they make it very easy for rescue boats to see the crew in the water.

Hull, made of polyurethane

Wooden rudder

Sprit

Mast, only as long as
the boat so it is easy
to transport

OLYMPIAN FEATS
These dinghies are
Olympic 470s, the most
popular of the Olympic
classes. This 4.7-m
(15-ft 5-in) boat was
designed in France. It
was introduced into the
Olympics to attract
young, light, and agile
sailors who could not
afford bigger dinghies

DARTING ABOUT
The dart is a catamaran, a twin hulled boat (p. 60).
Because these boats are so wide, they can carry a lot
of sail, so they are very fast and make for exciting
sailing. The dart has no centreboard or boom,
which keeps the cost down.

WET BOOTS
Like a wetsuit, dinghy
boots trap a film of water
between their inner surface
and the skin. The natural
warmth of the feet heats
this up so that it keeps
them warm.

Main sheet

Kicking strap, to keep
boom down

POINTLESS
For hands which are not
used to handling ropes,
gloves give protection as
well as warmth. These
gloves have no finger-
tips, so the wearer can
tie knots more easily
than with full gloves on.
They are made of a
synthetic material lined
with leather.

BEGINNER'S BOAT
This is a new plastic version of the most
popular training boat in the world, the Optimist
dinghy, first designed in the United States in 1948.
Originally the Optimist was popular because it
could be bought as a plywood kit and put together
at home. The boat's box-like shape made this very
easy to do. The layout and equipment are very
simple, making it an ideal boat for children as
young as seven to learn to sail in.

Daggerboard,
which slides up
and down, unlike
a centreboard
which pivots